IN THE NEOCLASSIC STYLE

IN THE NEOCLASSIC STYLE

Empire, Biedermeier and the Contemporary Home

Text by Melanie Fleischmann
Photographs by Mick Hales

Foreword by Richard Horn

THAMES AND HUDSON

A RUNNING HEADS BOOK
Copyright © 1988 by Running Heads Incorporated.
First published in the United States in 1988 by
Thames and Hudson Inc., 500 Fifth Avenue, New York,
New York 10110
Wallcovering border design by Jack Lindsay for Bayberry Handprints, Inc.
Location and furnishings for the photographs on pages 55, 63, 64, 65, 66 and
78, courtesy of Giles & Lewis.
All original photography by Mick Hales with the following exceptions:
National Gallery of Art/ Art Resource, p. 10
Kaveler/ Art Resource, p. 40
Geremy Butler Photography, p. 41

In The Neoclassic Style
was conceived and produced by
Running Heads Incorporated,
42 East 23rd Street,
New York, NY 10010

Library of Congress Catalog Card Number: 88-50191

Editor: Sarah Kirshner
Designer: Liz Trovato

Typeset by David E. Seham Associates
Color separation by Hong Kong Scanner Craft Company
Printed and bound in Singapore by Times Publishing Group.

DEDICATION

For Jane, who could, and did, sway the course of this project with the wave of a wonderful, tiny hand, and for her father, who puts things, as much as is possible, back on course.

ACKNOWLEDGMENTS

Once again, Polly Apfelbaum-Allen has labored cheerfully through thick and thin to achieve the impossible. She goes by the title of my assistant — it ought to be the other way around. Thank you, Polly.

Unending thanks, as always, to the designers, decorators, and architects whose hard work and talent gives us something to write about, and to their patrons, who put up with our invading their homes with our cameras. And a very special thank you to Edgar Mayhew, who allowed us, under what must have been trying circumstances, to photograph his home.

Thanks to Mick Hales, whose sure eye for style, symmetry and light enabled us to grace this book with some of the most lovely pictures ever taken of neoclassic interiors; to Liz Trovato, whose design made words and pictures into an elegant whole; to Jill Herbers whose enthusiasm and hard work at the beginning and the end of this undertaking gave it shape and life, and to Cornelia Guest, Susan Dwyer, Mary Forsell and numerous others whose skill and advice were invaluable on this project. Thanks also to Giles Forman and the staff of Giles & Lewis. And to Marta Hallett, Ellen Milionis, Sarah Kirshner and everyone at Running Heads, many thanks indeed.

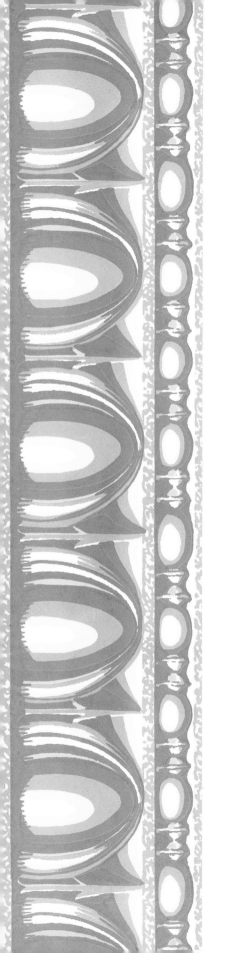

CONTENTS

CHAPTER FOUR
page 59

Neoclassic Accents and Objects

THE ORIGINALS AND THE UPDATES

CHAPTER FIVE
page 99

In the Neoclassic Style THE CONTEMPORARY HOME

CHAPTER SIX
page 123

The New Neo

FOREWORD

The final chapter of this book is entitled "The New Neo." The very term suggests, with its double prefix, a sense of ongoing, inexhaustible renewability. In this case it is the renewability of the classical style, a style that has been with us for over a thousand years and is still going strong, as the content of Melanie Fleischmann's book makes abundantly clear. Just why classicism is having yet another resurgence today has no simple answer. For many of today's architects and designers as well as for those who purvey or commission their creations, classicism's appeal, clearly, is boundless. It is a vein that can be mined over and over without giving out, one capable of offering inspiration in a way unrivaled by other styles.

"New Neo": the term implies an up-to-the-second yet traditional style which is, for many, an ideal compromise. Indeed, as seems to be the case, if design-conscious Americans seek a rooted but unstodgy tradition in this zero-gravity era, then surely "new neo" classicism provides what they are looking for. At the very least it provides the *look* of tradition, with buildings, furniture, and furnishings that offer themselves as the crispest and the freshest, and are, at the same time, a continuation of a mode of design that has been practiced in the West for centuries.

In our century of horrifying cataclysms and fast-paced social and economic changes, the traditions of the past remain, for many, something to grasp onto and live by. In the fields of design and architecture, however, tradition was more or less abolished by modernism. Modernists of the first half of the twentieth century, inspired by technological and industrial advances and the potential they offered to design, wanted to be faithful to the spirit of the new times and start over from scratch (although many of them were more beholden to the classical past than might have been supposed). But the results of starting anew offered cold comfort. People craved roots, which modernism seemed to lack. An alternative was needed. And so, starting around the mid-1960s, architects and designers sought these roots in classicism. Classicism, some architects believed (in Europe as well as in the United States), would furnish an ostensible and universally acknowledged tradition; the very thing that modernism had failed to supply.

Consequently, not only classical proportions (which were based, in fact, on *human* proportions, and were therefore considered more humane than the scaleless abstractions of modern architecture and design), but classical details as well, have come to sound, once again, an appealing note. And with the renewed interest in all forms of classicism, and the wide availability of monographs on the works of such seminal figures in the classical pantheon as Palladio, Boulle, Ledoux, Schinkel, and the Beaux-Arts architects (not to mention those on the great monuments of Greek and Roman antiquity), there has also come a resurgence of many of the crafts that once were used to enhance classical and neoclassical designs. The pared-down "new neo" classicism of the 1980s proves particularly alluring in that it endows the pristine geometries of modernism with elements that ring out with a sense of history.

"New Neo" holds an immediate appeal in the sheer pleasure we can take in its well-balanced proportions and logical order — hallmarks of the classical style. Even when classicism is distorted or cartooned, as it sometimes is in "new neo," its forms are still pleasing to the eye (and pleasing, too, to the satirically oriented mind that may enjoy the sight of fun being poked at a grand, if not to say grandiose, style). Surely it is the visual pleasure it provides that has assured classical design — both recently conceived "new neo" examples of it, as well as the earlier ones (Empire and Biedermeier furniture, for instance) that are so coveted today — of its continuing appeal.

This venerable style has an undeniable aura of power about it. In looking at the social significance of the "new neo" classicism that has arisen from this reassessment of classical traditions, we would do well to remember whose tradition is being invoked. It is striking that, in today's wildly diverse American culture, it should be *classicism* that has been hit upon as the style embodying tradition with a capital "T." Whose tradition, one wonders. If classicism is a *tradition* for anyone in America, it is for that American who is white, rich, and university educated. No wonder, then, that classicism — *the* style of the Western world's powerful — is an eminently conservative style. As such, perhaps classicism proves a model well suited to our politically and socially conservative period. No wacky boomerangs or desert orange-and-chartreuse interiors for the late 1980s (at least not for most of its designers, with notable exceptions: witness Memphis Milano and Atelier Alchimia in Milan, the witty Fifties revivalism in some of Alan Buchsbaum's late work, the brash, colorful designs of Arquitectonica, or the subtle buildings, interiors, and furniture of Christopher Alexander and his collaborators); rather, the classical has the look of timeless, uncontestable dignity and superiority, even if, given the political and economic realities of the late twentieth century, our supposed national superiority becomes a little less convincing by the year.

In addition to the political conservatism of the times, with "new neo" we may also have reached a "new" conservatism in architecture and design. Perhaps the faith in a glamorous, liberating modernity, or at least the enthusiasm for it that infused popular styles such as Art Deco and Fifties Modern, may have given way to a wish to recreate a past which is valued as a nobler, somehow better, time.

Still, if late 1980s economics played their part in fostering a congenial environment for a simplified "new neo" classicism, the appreciation for the originals on which "new neo" is based is ever growing. Preservationists throughout the United States fight hard to save myriad extant examples of classical and neoclassic architecture from the wrecking ball, whether it be the serene Greek Revival buildings of America's early years, or the more flamboyant Beaux-Arts edifices of the Gilded Age. And, as noted above, interest in Empire and Biedermeier antiques runs high (Biedermeier pieces are especially suited to today's tastes; they are at once monumental and playfully toylike, traditional looking but also spare enough to blend with modern designs). Even if, in all likelihood, we will never be able to duplicate the elements of the tradition out of which "new neo" springs except on a relatively small scale (for instance, the lovingly, patiently executed Pompeiian-style murals seen in many of today's urban residential and restaurant interiors), we can still appreciate and maintain those elements that have survived over the years, and still find much to admire, not only in them, but in our inventive updatings of them.

Richard Horn

INTRODUCTION

P hilip Johnson has said that there is only one absolute rule in the arts today: the inevitability of change. He should know. That this single architect could have created both the landmark modernist 1949 Glass House *and* its antithesis, the 1984 arcaded and pediment-capped AT&T headquarters, proves Johnson's claim, at least for the world of architecture.

While changing views on architecture affect the look of our buildings, the protean world of design and decoration is altering the look of our interiors. We have seen a swing away from the strict forms of high tech, functionalism, and minimalism to the playful designs of Memphis and the exuberant interiors of English-country and Victorian styles. Change is taking place once again as, more and more, we see a distillation of all these styles and forms, a return to the source of them all — a revival of the classical.

Classical forms — fluted columns and *klismos* chairs, the ancient symbols of lyres and acanthus leaves, the pleasing lines of pediments and amphorae — have had a way of reappearing from time to time ever since the Greeks gave them to us in about the fourth century B.C. (There is a reason, after all, that something enduring is called a classic.) Read through any art-history book and it is the classical you will encounter most often, returning in different artistic periods in various guises. In the centuries after the Greeks invented it, the classical became the fundamental style of ancient Rome, of the Renaissance, and of the baroque period. It reemerged in eighteenth-century England's Neo-Palladianism, in nineteenth-century Napoleonic France's Empire, England's Regency, Germany's Biedermeier, and America's Greek and Colonial Revivals. Today's "change," then, belongs to a great tradition of returning to the classical: the style called upon so often as a response to more excessive styles that get out of hand — a purifier, as it were.

If there is one classical revival in particular to which the current neoclassicism is indebted, then it is Empire. The style of Napoleon, for all its richness, is strikingly modern, for its forms are restrained to an almost Bauhausian degree. This par-

Left: Napoleon in His Study, *1810–11 by Jacques-Louis David. National Gallery of Art, Washington. The French emperor stands in front of some magnificent Empire pieces. The gilding and the massive lion's-head supports of the table display the craftsmanship of the emperor's own style.*

ticular manifestation of the classical had its beginnings in the last quarter of the eighteenth century, when, in a reaction to the elaborate ornamentation of rococo, the classical was tapped again as the style of choice. By 1804, when Napoleon declared himself emperor of France, neoclassicism was already very much in vogue. But it was a sweet, timid classicism compared to what it was to become in the hands of the new emperor.

Empire was one of the most enduring versions of the classical, more successful than the emperor himself at spreading influences throughout Western Europe, Russia, and America. The style had its infancy during the Directoire period — the final years of the Republic — and its dotage was during the reigns of Charles X and Louis Philippe, a scant half-century later. In the interim it spawned imitators all over the Western world. Because styles are part of a general artistic soup with no clear-cut beginnings and endings, our nomenclature is necessarily imprecise. But generally, the style that began in Paris came to be called Regency in England, Federal in the United States, and Empire through most of Europe. Germany and Austria had their very own, mostly unadorned, everyman's Empire called Biedermeier. And it is this group of styles that is making design waves again today.

The latest return to neoclassicism has, of course, its own contemporary touch. Once again, the need for change coincides with the need for purification. From the numerous classical revivals preceding our own, however, today's designers have many sources from which to cull their ideas, rather than responding to the dictates of an emperor. The result is a classicism with great spirit — classic lines mixing equally well with luxuriant Empire-period fabrics, Pompeiian-style frescoes, and modern icons like the Tizio lamp. Classic shapes are being produced in the latest alloys and materials as well as being recreated in lovely Biedermeieresque wood finishes.

Neoclassicism has never amounted to a mere fad, and the pretext of this book is not to highlight it as one. Nor is this book meant to be a scholarly treatise, as many facets of the revival of classical themes in art, architecture, and design have been exhaustively explored elsewhere. Rather, it is intended to be a brief, and hopefully entertaining and informative, investigation of the appeal of the classical style — its strength and symmetry — with a focus on the Empire style and its spinoffs. Classical themes are just that — classic — and they will be here in one fashion or another for a while. Long enough, in any event, to make it worthwhile to explore how the design world is handling the classical this time around.

CHAPTER
ONE

THE EMPEROR'S NEW STYLE

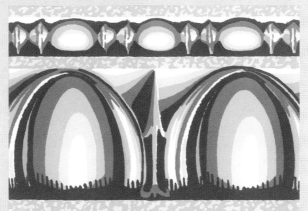

T HE EMPEROR'S NEW STYLE

When Napoleon appointed himself emperor of France in 1804, he became the ruler of a nation whose decorative arts were floundering in post-

Revolutionary disarray. France had thrown herself from monarchy to democracy to empire in a quick fifteen years, and the upper classes who had once been patrons of the decorative arts were — if they still retained their heads — hardly in a position to hire artisans to furnish magnificent houses. Nor had they been replaced.

Still, the artists and craftsmen who had been responsible for the magnificent decorative arts of the Bourbon monarchy had not vanished — it only remained for someone to put their talents to use. That someone, of course, was the emperor himself, and his call was for a style that would symbolize the glory of the empire that he envisioned.

This task was accomplished in spades. The style that emerged in response to the dictates of the emperor is probably more completely and more enduringly striking than its designers ever anticipated. And though the beginnings of Empire can be seen in the furniture made during the Directoire period and even prior to it, the Empire period was the pinnacle of this stylistic movement.

Napoleon not only eradicated the political vestiges of the republicanism for which so much blood had been shed, he also would have none of its symbols. Out went the decorative motifs of the Republic: the oak, the pikes, the tricolor, the cap of Liberty, the level, and the three clasped hands of Liberty, Equality, and Fraternity. In came the motifs of the ancient Greeks — the lyre, the star, and the lozenge — and motifs from Roman, Egyptian, Pompeiian, and Etruscan art — sphinxes, palmettes, chimeras, caryatids, and winged heads of lions, dolphins, and swans. Gone also was the delicacy of the furnishings made during the final years of the monarchy, superseded by work that was simple, rectilinear, and at the same time wonderfully grandiose. Though Empire borrowed from all the civilizations of antiquity, it was toward the look of ancient Rome that the style gravitated most. After all, the style of Caesar befitted an emperor far more than the style of the democratic Greeks.

Right: The suite of tigerwood furniture in this neoclassic interior displays the inlaid wood typical of Empire and related styles. The alabaster lamp in the shape of a column dates from the 1920s, while the print of the pyramid which hangs above the couch dates from the 1820s reflecting the classical references predominant in Empire and subsequent periods.

Left: The gilded opulence of the winged lions supporting this Biedermeier table reflect Napoleon's imperial influence on the decorative arts of the nineteenth century. The cultures of antiquity — especially Egypt and Rome — supplied the mythological imagery of winged lions, sphinxes, chimeras, dolphins and swans.

Left: The painted-wood bookshelves in this New York apartment are an imaginative "new-neo" use of that time-honored classic the fluted column. Columns were an important decorative feature in Empire design borrowed, of course, from ancient Greece and Rome.

*Right: This columned desk domi-
nates the workspace of designer Michael Kreiger. Modern representa-
tions of classical columns hold up
what appears to be a miniature
Parthenon in the Empire tradition
of using columns as table supports.
The desk is made of painted wood,
and the chair behind it is from the
Empire period.*

OLD AS NEW *The two artists who are generally credited with creating the Empire style are Charles Percier and Pierre-François-Leonard Fontaine. They were architects, and admirers of antiquity*

to such a degree that, as students at the French Royal Academy in Rome, they had earned the moniker "the Etruscans." In the preface to their book *Recueil de décorations intérieures* (1801–1812), Percier and Fontaine wrote, "It is a delusion to believe that there are shapes preferable to those which the ancients have handed down to us." And so, when Napoleon commissioned them to redecorate and refurnish Josephine's palace, Malmaison, it was to the ancients that they turned for inspiration.

Percier and Fontaine were not copyists. Even though excavations were going on at Herculaneum and Pompeii throughout the second part of the eighteenth century, access to the sites was nearly impossible to attain. While most of the excavated material available for study was in Rome, still, in terms of actual furniture, there was a paucity of ancient examples. So Percier and Fontaine drew from the classical as it suited them, hybridizing that with contemporary forms, and, as a result, producing a style that was splendidly original.

Their other great source was ancient Egypt. While Napoleon's Egyptian campaign of 1798 to 1799 might not have been a complete military success, culturally it was enormously influential — a gold mine of design ideas. The archaeologist, architect, and artist Baron Dominique Vivant de Denon joined the Egyptian campaign and returned to France to publish the two-volume *Voyages dans la basse et la haute Égypte* in 1802. With 141 plates, this great stylistic sourcebook helped make terminal figures of lotus, lily, and papyrus flowers; date palms and reeds; the sphinx; lotus capitals; and lion's head supports for chairs and tables, part of the decorative palette.

Many of these Egyptian motifs overlapped the styles appropriated from ancient Greece and Rome, which was only logical, for the ancient Greeks had borrowed largely from Egypt, and Rome had taken what it wanted from Greece. Down the line, each civilization had put its own stamp on what it had plundered, and the French were no exception. Empire furniture built upon the overall grandeur of the Romans, took decorative ideas from

Left: The view at the top of the stairway of the same apartment by Saladino looks like a beautifully restored Pompeiian ruin complete with columns, artifactlike urns, and verdigris stair rail.

Right: The apartment embodies an intriguing mixture of ancient Roman classicism and Empire-style neoclassicism. At left is the imposing classic shape of the column, and at right is a glimpse of the refinement and softness of a neoclassic interior.

Left: Like Percier and Fontaine, the two architects who created Empire style for Napoleon, today's designers draw from the classical, combining it with contemporary forms to produce splendidly original designs. John Saladino borrows the shape and surface of the column to create a massive architectural element for this apartment.

the whole ancient world, and used forms both ancient and contemporary.

What Percier and Fontaine created for Napoleon was based on something antique, but the style was a complete invention, which was why it was so successful. Things have changed surprisingly little. Today's neoclassicism would be noticed by relatively few had it not attracted the attention of the design trade. To them goes the credit for taking an artifact and making it work in a contemporary setting.

The current favor of Empire also has a lot to do with the quality of what is really a wonderful style. Empire has a little something for every part of the human psyche. There are carved mythological beasts to captivate the child in all of us, gilded appliqués to delight those of us who are magpies, and the unsurpassed craftsmanship, balance, and design it takes to please those of us who are cognoscenti. One would be hard pressed to find another style that is so completely gratifying.

To this end a remarkable variety of crafts were often used

Left: The craftsmanship of Empire and related styles is displayed beautifully in the use of exotic wood veneers and inlays. The pattern on this drop-front desk is a stylized lotus blossom surrounded by palm fronds sitting in a vase.

for a single piece. The outstanding workmanship of the period probably had to do with the fact that, until they were abolished in 1791, the guilds had restricted each workshop to one specialty. With guilds gone, it was far easier for one shop to produce a complicated piece that required many areas of expertise.

In 1803, for example, the Jacob brothers employed craftsmen working at fifteen different trades, all to do with the production of furniture. There were painters, carvers, gilders, wood joiners and turners, metal gilders, bronze founders, and more.

For every different craft associated with Empire furniture, there were several, if not countless, design motifs. Columns, for instance, are a signature of classicism, and Empire cabinetmakers incorporated them into many of their designs. Tables rested on them, mirrors were supported by them, and chests of drawers and other case pieces were flanked by them. But, if columns weren't quite right for the piece, chances are that pilasters were. And what columns and pilasters didn't support, caryatids, sphinxes, or carved animal figures — plain, or gilded — did.

Similarly, Empire cabinetmakers chose from an endless list of materials. The Romans had had an affection for exotic woods and wood veneers, and the French were no different. Apart from mahogany, they used lemon wood, elm, ash, walnut, yew, and ebony, to name but a few. They also inlaid contrasting woods, as well as materials such as silver, pewter, and mother of pearl; in addition their use of decorative mounts, especially those of gilt bronze, has probably never been equalled. In fact, the more rare a material, the more likely that it would be somehow incorporated into the Empire interior. Steel was a case in point. A rare metal at the time, what wasn't used for weaponry was used for some of the most beautiful furniture of the period. It was decorated in much the same manner as wooden furniture: inlaid with other metals, accented with gilt bronze, and topped with marble. Depending on how it was tempered, it could be given different colored patinas — violet, green, blue, red, and black; and, because of its inherent strength, it could be used to make furniture of great grace, though of course still based on the same classical influences. Though we often think of cold stones as materials for classical pieces and smooth woods for neoclassic ones, metals have strong associations with both styles because they were used with such appreciation and were employed whenever they could be obtained.

With all its complexities, it is not surprising that there are a handful of misconceptions about neoclassic furniture and decor. Many people feel that it is formidable and unapproach-

Above: In this contemporary home designed by architect Michael Graves, we can see the column imagery of classicism echoed in the wood supports of the torchères and the fluting of the marble fireplace. The lyre-backed chair is an Empire-period design.

able, fine only for museums and perhaps high style (read "overdone") interiors. Others find it elegant and covetable, but alas, about as appropriate in a contemporary setting as white lace gloves at a cookout. Lastly, it is categorized as unaffordable. All of which assumptions are untrue.

The reality is that the neoclassic achieves the impossible: It embodies two completely contradictory approaches. Its basic forms are restrained, strict, even sleek, true to their classical roots. Strip an Empire chair of its gilded appliqués and you have a piece that is strikingly refined, and — dare it be said — strikingly modernist. Aficionados of Biedermeier can attest to that. Those same Empire appliqués, however, point to the more opulent side of the neoclassic; the gilded dolphins, lion's heads, and carved paw feet turning a pared-down form into a decorative tour de force.

All told, Empire, Regency, Biedermeier, and their modern interpretations are stylistic chameleons. Decorative as they are, they have been found to work in a ranch house, perfectly comfortable amid straw matting and cool white linen slipcovers. They are equally at home with the strict restraint of Breuer or with the happy excesses of Buatta.

As far as being unaffordable goes, what popularity might have caused, popularity has solved. For starters, although some of the original French Empire pieces have stratospheric price tags, many don't, and numerous Empire-offshoot styles also remain at earthbound prices. Secondly, contemporary furniture designers and manufacturers have not been caught napping. Some of the most interesting furniture collections to be put together in years are either reproductions or spin-offs of Empire and Empire-related styles. All of which brings Empire and its friends, whether crafted in carved and gilded wood or formed in glass and steel, within an affordable range.

Right: This house, designed by Bob Patino and Vicente Wolf, combines contemporary glass and steel with the elegance of nineteenth-century wood columns to create refined, restrained neoclassicism.

Left: From the camel on the tablecloth to the place settings with architectural patterns, this room designed by Patino and Wolf is a bracing display of contemporary neoclassicism. Additional touches include the classically fluted vase and glasses and the bust placed atop a reproduction Regency oak table with columns for legs.

CHAPTER
TWO

A PORTFOLIO OF IMPERIAL STYLES

BIEDERMEIER
By the end of Napoleon's reign, most of continental Europe, and Russia as well, had adopted the Empire style. It varied only slightly from state to state, and it was all clearly recognizable

for what it was. In Vienna, however, something slightly different was brewing, even at the very beginning of the nineteenth century. By 1814, when the Congress of Vienna filled the town with the diplomats and princes who were to ponder the fate of post-Napoleonic Europe, the style in Vienna had become developed enough to make some of those men want to take pieces of furniture home with them.

The Congress of Vienna could be said to mark the end of one extension of Empire and the beginning of another, which was to become known as Biedermeier. The name — *bieder* 'plain' and *Meier*, a common German surname — was coined to mock the developing middle class, and insinuated that their comfortable way of life — their parlor games and friendly gossip — left no room for creativity or imagination.

Whether or not the moniker is an accurate social appraisal, it is not completely accurate when it comes to design. The term has come to encapsulate all Austrian, German, and even some Scandinavian furniture from about 1810 to 1860, which is certainly when the style existed. It is also assumed to describe plain, functional furniture for the middle class. But some of the furniture was hardly suited for middle-income earners, especially some of the early, very elaborate pieces, and very little of it can be categorized as plain.

Generally, Biedermeier furniture is recognizable for its broad expanses of beautiful pale-colored veneer and its contrasting dark inlays of ebony or ebonized wood. All of this cloaks what is usually an identifiable Empire form.

The gilt-bronze appliqués are for the most part missing, which had more to do with a disaffection for all things Napoleonic than a weakness on the part of Viennese craftsmen. They had proved themselves quite capable, but the market for that kind of decoration, and anything else that might seem grandiose, was drying up.

Before the demand vanished completely, however, some wonderful transitional pieces were made. They were a mix of

Opposite: Viennese craftsmen usually inlaid the pale-wood veneers of Biedermeier furniture with ebony rather than the more expensive and more ornate ormolu used by the French. These chairs display the pleasing contrast of dark and light that was the Biedermeier trademark.

Left: The curved high-backed sofa and Austrian walnut-veneer secretaire with ebony inlay shown in this library are sterling examples of Biedermeier craftsmanship.

Empire forms and flat surfaces, gilded carving and bronze appliqués, with voluptuous rococo curves. One example is a secretaire, made in about 1810 in Vienna. The whole is shaped like a lyre and is about five feet tall. The front presents a completely flat, mahogany-veneered surface, with distinctly Empire bronze mounts. The flap, which pulls down to become the writing surface, is at the widest part and is flanked by gilded and winged female figures. Beneath the flap are three drawers, where the piece tapers to an almost impossibly narrow waist. Then the piece flares outward again, terminating in a flourish of gilded acanthus leaves, carved paw feet, and a hefty pedestal.

As changing tastes prevented Biedermeier cabinetmakers from using rich ornament, they made up for it by coming up with extraordinary and often wildly impractical forms. A chest of drawers from just a few years later than the secretaire presents a flat rectilinear surface from the front, but in profile the whole piece is S-scrolled, bulging largely at the top, receding in the middle, and sweeping outwards again at the bottom to end in a neat little ducktail. Apart from the discreet outline carving at the ends of the scrolls, and gilt-bronze escutcheons, the piece is all flat, unadorned mahogany veneer. Still, it can hardly be said to be restrained or stolid.

Typical of the Biedermeier style were secretaires of massive proportion, topped with complex superstructures, and sofas with high backs and elaborately scrolled armrests. For these as well as other pieces of furniture, commonly used woods were cherry, ash, birch, pear, and walnut. And although beautifully grained veneer accounted for most of the decoration, supports in the form of dolphins, swans, griffins, and the like were not unheard of, nor were the vast majority of Empire decorative motifs. Their manifestation, however, was different. They were inlaid, painted, or — more rarely — stenciled onto the veneer, or interpreted in carved wood or plaster. Such gilding as there was went onto that carving, but just as often, carved features were of wood that was chosen for its attractive grain. And increasingly, as culture chose to forget the warlike Napoleonic era, naturalistic motifs such as butterflies, flowers, and even hearts, appeared.

If Biedermeier marked the beginning of design for the middle class, it also, as a result, marked the beginning of furniture that was more adaptable. The typical Biedermeier householder did not hire an architect to build his house, let alone furniture for his rooms. Furthermore, furniture was no longer strictly limited to a position against a wall — it might be put anywhere, and moved from place to place as needs dictated. So for the most part, furniture could not be built as an architectural component.

With the advent of machinery in the 1830s, thin strips of wood could be bent, glued together in a single curve, and then veneered. The result was that furniture designs became increasingly sinuous. Michael Thonet based his factory on this process, and although his chairs and those of other factories were mass-produced, they maintained, at first, the veneered flat surfaces and basic forms of Biedermeier design. But gradually furniture design in the German-speaking countries, as elsewhere, was to proceed into the Victorian age. Restraint on all fronts was to disappear, superseded by an apparent drive to embellish whatever could possibly be embellished, and to fill every vacant space with something, be it functional or no.

Right: Like the Biedermeier style, these contemporary pieces designed by Michael Graves are influenced by both the classic and the neo-classic. The chairs are based on classic forms, while the bird's-eye-maple veneer and ebonized-wood inlay are clearly elements of a modern interpretation of Biedermeier design.

ENGLAND AND THE REGENCY

The Regency was a period which ran politically from 1811 to 1820, while the Prince of Wales (later George IV) was acting as regent for his ailing father,

George III. Stylistically, it spans the quarter century from about 1795 to 1820, and, even though the two nations were at war for all but seven of those years, it was a style that came to England almost solely from France.

The English had been toying with classicism throughout the later eighteenth century. But like the classicism of Louis XVI's France, it was the charming little sister of the style that was to follow. When the Empire influence began to land on their shores, the English were living in houses influenced — both inside and out — by the designs of the architects James and Robert Adam. They were certainly classically inspired. But there were still vestiges of the baroque and rococo floating around, and, especially when it came to interiors, a certain delicacy and curvaceousness. There was also a fascination with things Chinese — to wit, the Prince of Wales's Chinese drawing room, made for his Carlton House by the architect Henry Holland in the 1780s.

But China was not all that influenced Henry Holland. In fact, if there was a single early conduit for French design ideas, it was Henry Holland. He not only borrowed from the Directoire style, he also purchased many a French piece of furniture. Furthermore, he had Carlton House decorated almost entirely by French craftsmen.

Holland's successor in the role was Thomas Hope. A close friend and admirer of Percier's, Hope deplored current English taste. He had spent a great deal of time traveling in Greece, Syria, Egypt, and Sicily, and his preferred interior was more akin to the ancient ones he had seen in his travels, which meant, broadly speaking, with less ornamentation. Being a well-off banker, he could and did take it upon himself to bring the rest of England around to his way of thinking.

Hope decorated his house on Duchess Street in London to his own designs, and then let in streams of visitors. In 1807 he published a book of the designs from the house, called *Household Furniture and Interior Decoration.* A year later, the equally influential

Left: X-form stools, like this authentic piece, were highly fashionable in the Regency period. The form is from the ancient Greeks, but the gilding is purely Regency.

Above: This English Regency rosewood table has a classical frieze on its surface typical of the period. The lion-mask ornaments and paw feet are also characteristic of the style. The chairs on either side are nineteenth-century copies of Adam.

London cabinetmaker George Smith published his similarly titled *Collection of Designs for Household Furniture and Interior Decoration.* Both of these books were laden with the influence of French Empire, and with designs gleaned from ancient bas-relief carvings, bronze sculptures, and paintings on vases.

The English had always been great collectors, and the assimilation of a style, even if it came from an arch-rival, was not something they found offensive. Furthermore, classical decor was well suited to the display of classical antiquities, a collection of which existed in more than a few important English households. Empire, with its emphasis on a perceived Grecian ideal, was welcomed as part of an ongoing interest in things classical. At the same time, its form, with an emphasis on symmetry, and its strict formality, were novel enough to be intriguing.

Regency furniture was, for the most part, very much like the French Empire furniture that inspired it. The favored woods were mahogany and rosewood, although more exotic woods were also used. Satinwood was often used for inlay and stringing. Just as in France, wood was carved into various forms, and was gilded and painted.

Bronze, brass, and copper were used decoratively as well, for surface mounts, inlays, and often, when a lyre-form was used, for its strings. Some pieces had pierced metal galleries or metal paw feet; other furniture had doors made of brass trellises, backed by silk. Drawers had small brass or bronze knobs, ornamented or plain — often a lion mask with a ring pull. The English also made furniture out of steel, although because the metal was rare, the furniture was equally so.

The English were the first to move their furniture away from the wall, where it had theretofore been placed, and arrange it in the middle of the room, around the fireplace, for example. Previously, although furniture might have been moved away from the walls during the course of a social gathering, it would never have been left there. A Frenchman, on seeing such an arrangement at Osterley Park, was horrified and reportedly referred to the room as "dérangée." Dérangée or no, it foreshadowed the start of the Victorian penchant for studiously haphazard rooms.

Left: In the foreground of this room full of furniture of various neoclassic styles is a Regency X-form bench. In typical Regency fashion, the bench is decorated with gilded rams' heads and paw feet.

AMERICA

At the end of the eighteenth century America was a newly minted democracy, infatuated with its political role model, Greece. Houses had begun to look like small Greek temples, and

furniture had already become neoclassically inspired in much the same sense as that of eighteenth century Europe and England. And, like that of its transatlantic peers, America's neoclassicism was pretty and delicate; but it was a restrained precursor of what it was to become.

Furniture in America at this stage drew largely from English designs, even with the end of the so-called Colonial period, and the establishment, in 1789, of the Federal government. The Federal period (the name is a catchall that includes Hepplewhite, Sheraton, and finally the Empire styles in America) saw the fading popularity of the rococo and chinoiserie designs of Thomas Chippendale, and the rise of the more neoclassic designs of Robert Adam, especially as they were interpreted in the late eighteenth-century design books of George Hepplewhite and Thomas Sheraton. By the 1820s the style that Napoleon had wrought was on the wane in France, while in America it was just reaching its peak.

It might have made sense had America rejected, on the grounds that Napoleon had overthrown the French democracy, all things Napoleonic. America had, after all, just fought a terrific war to free herself from a monarchy. But in America, just as in England, fashion paid no heed to politics, and so Empire style swept across the Atlantic. And politics aside, America had a great affection for the French. Louis XVI had, after all, supported the Americans in their revolutionary war, and his assistance doubtlessly helped make the revolutionaries the victors.

America celebrated the cause of the French revolutionaries, and in the War of 1812 considered herself an ally of Napoleon, for it was still premature to side with the British. So when Napoleon's brother Joseph Bonaparte moved to Philadelphia in 1815, he was warmly received, just as other French arrivals had been welcomed previously, regardless of their politics. Whatever the French brought with them, be it furnishings, fashions, or points of view, held great sway in American design, especially after the turn of the century.

Above: This is a house — a museum in fact — whose interior has been decorated to approximate an American interior from the 1820s. The sideboard is American and was made in 1825 and decorated with ormolu mounts and hardware.

The architect Benjamin Henry Latrobe was among the first Americans to practice the new style. He had worked in London, knew the work of Henry Holland, and was certainly aware of what was going on in France. He returned to America in 1795, and moved to Philadelphia, where he designed not only houses, but the furniture for them as well. All of his work showed the influence of historical classicism.

Latrobe's furniture designs, which might be viewed as a French original, modified by the English, and interpreted by an American — with a little influence from antiquity thrown in for good measure — have a charm not to be found in their trans-atlantic cousins. The classical forms are there, as are the flat surfaces and the essentially rectilinear designs. But the gilt-bronze mounts are gone, replaced by painted and gilded gesso, the motifs having to do with conquests. The posturing animals have lost their place to foliage-derived designs, and the overall forms are less emphatically severe.

Furniture like Latrobe's was probably more similar to French Directoire furniture than Empire furniture, if one wants to be very analytical, and in fact some authorities refer to furniture made between about 1805 and 1815 as American Directoire.

Left: The master bedroom in the Deshon-Allyn House in New London, Connecticut. The sleigh bed is American Empire as is the chest of drawers. The wallpaper is a copy of French Empire paper from the nineteenth century.

Above: The South Parlor. The mahogany armchairs and side chair are in the style of Duncan Phyfe made by New York cabinetmaker Ernest Hager in the mid-nineteenth century. The curtain treatments are from an authentic early-nineteenth-century design.

But like French furniture, American furniture was to become progressively more massive and more elaborate as the Empire influence took hold.

Most American architects did not get involved in furniture design the way Latrobe did, so it was the cabinetmakers who interpreted and broadcast the new style. They scrutinized actual furniture that was imported from France and England, and pored over the design books of Thomas Hope, George Smith, Percier and Fontaine, and the like. Then they constructed their furniture using locally available material.

Decorative motifs such as shields, eagles, and the thirteen stars, which had been favorites in the new republic, were to remain in fashion. As the nineteenth century progressed, they were joined by motifs typical of the Empire style and were also reinterpreted in a more typically Empire mode. The eagle, once inlaid in contrasting wood within a modest oval medallion, became a massive carved and gilded figure. Likely as not, spangled banners streamed from his beak. The piece of furniture he adorned might well be supported by something more expected of a French piece, such as pilasters terminating in paw feet.

Some of the more prominent cabinetmakers working during the Empire period were Scottish-born Duncan Phyfe, who set up shop on Fulton Street in New York, and Thomas Wetherill and Joseph B. Barry in Philadelphia. There was also a group of French émigré cabinetmakers, notably Charles Honoré Lannuier in New York, and Anthony G. Quervelle and Michel Bouvier in Philadelphia. One important commission for Bouvier was the furnishing of Joseph Bonaparte's house.

The elaborate gilt-bronze mounts so typical of French Empire furniture were less common in American furniture. More likely to be found were motifs that were painted or stenciled on, or inlaid with a contrasting wood. Brass was also used decoratively, both on its own and in combination with ebony to form marquetry panels known as buhlwork or boulle. Knobs were often made of brass, stamped with designs, and later of glass, and later yet of wood.

Much of the decorative metal work that was used was imported, a process that could be complicated from time to time by political exigencies. Furthermore, it meant that the metal work was often not made for a specific piece of furniture — it was more likely the furniture was made to suit the metal work. Still, America didn't have centuries of monarchs in her past, patronizing and developing the kind of fabulous craftsmanship that Napoleon's cabinetmakers had at their disposal. So American furniture was perforce more simple.

Mahogany remained the wood of choice, but there were also native woods used such as maple, tulipwood, cherry, spruce, white pine, and cedar. More exotic woods like satinwood and ebony were used for borders and inlaying, and in some cases one wood was painted to resemble another, and then decorated.

Left: The Deshon-Allyn House was built in 1829. The hallway displays more of the superb collection of American Empire–period furnishings. The small bench at the end of the hall has a swan's-head motif matching that of the chair in the master bedroom.

Right: This American sofa is upholstered in red velvet. Crafted around 1830, it has mounts made of ormolu.

CHAPTER
THREE

NEOCLASSIC FURNITURE:
THE ORIGINALS AND THE UPDATES

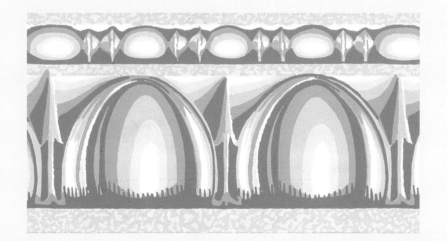

SEATING Percier and Fontaine are, of course, an important part of the tradition of furniture designed by architects and designers. In the same vein are Regency designers Robert Adam and Thomas Hope, and in this century Jacques-Émile Ruhlmann, Marcel Breuer, Le Corbusier, and Ludwig Mies van der Rohe, to mention but a few. It is a prestigious group, and judging by the number of architects and designers now trying their hands at furniture design, it is a group whose ranks are going to swell substantially in the future.

And even if the new furniture is not designed, as was that of Percier and Fontaine, for specific places in specific rooms, it still owes much to the neoclassic tradition. The motifs that Percier and Fontaine borrowed from ancient Greece, Rome, and Egypt are with us again, whether employed for a familiar purpose or one wholly novel. Many are the new designs in polished steel, some embellished with brass or bronze, some patinated to a lovely weathered green.

One of the most typical pieces of the Empire period, to the modern eye, at least, is the *bateau en lit* or daybed. The *bateau en lit* form shines through in countless modern beds, sofas, and chaise longues. Its ancient precedents were generally more delicate pieces, with turned and tapering legs. Though not massive, these couches were hardly without embellishment — there are examples with bone carvings, silver and glass inlay, lion masks, horse heads, human masks, and so forth.

But the Empire interpretation has far more verve. Broad expanses of flat surface are a mark of the style, and, in a piece as large as the *bateau en lit,* this is wonderfully evident. The sides of these beds look as though they were stamped from a plank, and when they intersect with headboards and footboards, they do so at sharp right angles. Ornament is, plentiful, but it is applied to flat surfaces. Rarely is any carving or embellishment put where it would soften an angle or interfere with a deliberately sharp, clear-cut silhouette.

Perhaps the most famous of these beds, and one that gave us yet another name for the form, is that of Madame Récamier, designed in 1798 by the architect Louis-Martin Berthault, who was a pupil of Percier and Fontaine. The bed (which might actually have been designed by Percier), was built by the famed Jacob brothers of mahogany and decorated with gilt-bronze swans, classical figures, and other motifs. Its hangings were white muslin, spangled with stars and fringed. Behind it there was a large mirror panel, behind which the wall was draped with violet silk, edged in black and capped with a buff-colored gold-bordered silk pelmet. The whole composition was set in an arched niche, and the final effect created a sensation in Paris.

Madame Récamier's bed, established in the archives of art history by the famous portrait by Jacques-Louis David, falls officially into the Directoire period. With the maturing of the Empire style, the form was to become even more elaborate and often far less delicate. A bed made for the Empress Josephine after 1810 by Jacob-Desmalter et Cie (a later evolution of the Jacob brothers firm) had massive carved swans flanking the headboard, rectangular sides covered with carved motifs, and was gilded from head to cornucopia-shaped toe.

Right: The Bed of Madame Récamier, *1802 by Robert Smirke. The British Architectural Library, RIBA, London. This watercolor rendering shows the bed that created a sensation in Empire Paris. The muslin and silk hangings and the elaborate decoration of the mahogany bed are impressive even today.*

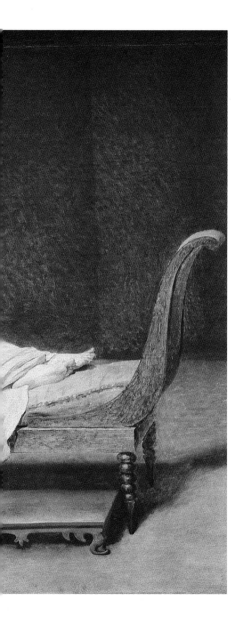

Left: Madame Récamier, *circa 1793 by Jacques-Louis David. Louvre Museum, Paris. The daybed or couch, designed in the classical style, was an exceedingly fashionable piece of Empire furniture. Madame Récamier is perched upon its milder Directoire precursor.*

Opposite: The bench in the foreground exhibits all the properties of
the Empire style: a large expanse
of space, scrolled arms, and gold-
leaf gilding.

Right: This little love seat is a
modified version of the bateau en
lit that is well suited to its simple
contemporary setting.

Right: There is no mistaking the authenticity of this lovely gold-and-black-painted English sofa made circa 1810 and well situated in its New London, Connecticut, period setting. The scrolled arms and curved legs are an example of the modified Empire bateau en lit form that found its source in the beds and couches of ancient Greece and Rome.

Below: Though this sofa displays all the earmarks of an unusual Empire piece, with its classical lines, frieze decorating the front, and steel construction, it is a 1980s "new neo" piece designed by Peter Carlson that captures Empire elegance in a fresh way.

Above: Fringes and tassels are an Empire-style decorative element found on this contemporary sofa that displays a classical lineage with its outward curving arm. The leopard skin adds an exotic touch to what is a classically simple design scheme.

CHAIRS

If there is one irresistible urge all architects and designers seem to have at some stage in their careers, it is to design furniture. Chairs in particular seem to be the item of choice for furniture design. It has been said that this is because a chair is perhaps the quintessential mixture of functional design and visual art.

Two ancient forms which were transplanted into the late eighteenth and early nineteenth century and are clearly discernible in new chairs designed today are the *klismos* and the *thronos*, chairs whose basic shapes became the reference points for most of the chairs of the Napoleonic era. The *klismos* was a Greek design of the fifth century B.C., with backward-sweeping rear legs that merged into forward-curved back supports, so that in profile the chair legs and back formed a shallow "S." The front legs, mirror images of the back legs, curved forward, and often the uprights rolled over, terminating in swan's heads or some other decorative carving. The backrest was rectangular, resting on top of, instead of between, the back supports, which meant that it would make contact with the chair's occupant at about the shoulder blades.

The Empire interpretations of the *klismos* are quickly recognizable. But classical or not, no form escaped modification. Thus, often the saber-shaped front legs were forfeited in favor of a turned vertical design, or the forward sweep of the back supports disappeared and the whole back of the chair, from floor to top of chair back, was in profile a shallow, backward-facing "C" curve.

The *thronos* was a chair that the Greeks assigned to deities and royalty (hence our word *throne*). It borrowed not only from the Egyptians, but from the Etruscans. It came with paw feet, with the entire chair leg carved in imitation of an animal's leg, and with legs and sometimes arms in the form of a sphinx or some winged animal. There were rectangular and turned legs, variously carved, and there were legs that vanished entirely in favor of solid underframing that went all the way to the floor.

The Romans took both of these Greek chair forms, especially the *thronos*, and adapted them to their own taste, and generally their taste ran towards the grandiose. From Rome the chairs voyaged to Napoleonic France, grandiosity unscathed. The *klismos*-inspired chairs retained a certain delicacy — the essentially curvaceous and insubstantial nature of the form saw to that. But the *thronos* was to become highly elaborate and hybridized with other designs so that in some cases it was barely recognizable as its original classic form.

Below: The arms of these nineteenth-century French dining chairs terminate in swans' heads. To the right of the door is a "Toscana" tub chair, based on the thronos, designed for Sapporiti Italia.

Right: Though new, this chair is unmistakably Empire in form with its sloping arms, straight back, and tailored legs. The wheat motif in the chair back is not strictly Empire, though its placement and crafts-manship are in the Empire spirit.

A gilded throne chair designed by Percier and Fontaine for Napoleon looks much like its Roman counterpart, with lion's-head supports, massive paw feet, and an arched rectangular back that merges with its solid underframing. Other Empire chairs have *klismos*-reminiscent S-shaped backs integrated into an upholstered armchair design. One such design by Percier, executed by the Jacob brothers, had carved, three-dimensional swans, painted white, as arms; saber-shaped front legs; and a curved, tub-shaped back. It was a successful mélange of Greek, Roman, and Etruscan ideas — not to mention contemporary European notions — all made into a completely original design.

In Austria, side chairs were probably the earliest and most astonishing Biedermeier pieces. They were no doubt based on the Empire *klismos* shape, and their legs were similarly tapered or saber-shaped. But their backs were completely divergent from mainstream Empire style. They were exuberantly curved, with back supports that often swept inward just about where one's waist would be, and then flared out again to join a crest rail that might have been any one of hundreds of fan-shaped, C-scrolled, swan-necked, or otherwise extraordinary designs. The C-scrolled crest rail had existed as far back as the reign of Louis XV in France, but it was then a controlled, demure, downward-curved detail — not at all like those conjured up by the chair makers of the Biedermeier period.

Right: This tiger-wood chair is a klismos *form with wood inlaid in classical patterns. It is upholstered in silk drapery fabric from the 1920s and is part of a suite of Biedermeier furniture in the New York home of Maureen Geiger.*

Left: This klismos-*form chair is Italian from the mid-nineteenth century. The serpent back is carved wood covered with gesso and gilding.*

Right: The Michael Graves dining room chair in the foreground is a latter-day interpretation of the *klismos* curve. The simplicity of its form looks well in a plain, unadorned setting.

Opposite: This chair is a Biedermeier antique with a horsehair cushion. The stool to the left was designed by Michael Graves for Diane von Furstenburg and complements its neoclassic ancestor beautifully.

TABLES

Other pieces of ancient furniture had also reappeared in France. The tripod table, with animal-shaped legs and either a flat or basin-shaped circular top, became the gueridon and the athénienne. There was plenty of furniture, however, that wasn't derived from ancient forms. Furniture from earlier periods was given a contemporary stamp and moved into the Empire repertoire. Console tables, which had four legs but were designed to have one side rest against a wall, were beautifully suited to the rectilinear form so characteristic of the period. Their front legs became, for example, tapering square pilasters, topped, perhaps, with caryatid heads and ending with gilded paw feet, or square pedestals.

Circular tables of about three or four feet in diameter, called tea or dining tables, were also perfect vehicles for Empire designs. Their variety was endless, and apart from the paw feet, varied inlays of exotic woods, bronze animal figures, and mounts of gilt and patinated bronze, many of the tables were topped with Sèvres porcelain plaques. Of all Empire furniture pieces, these tables are certainly the showstoppers.

A few words should be said here about table nomenclature. At the time, small, round, marble-topped tables were called gueridons, as were any other round tables without marble tops. Larger round tables with marble tops were known as tea tables and dining tables. Today, happily, the word gueridon seems to take care of any round table.

There were rectangular game tables, for backgammon and checkers, that had removable tops and converted into writing tables; jardinières; bedside tables; and toilet tables, which came equipped with basins, larger mirrors, and candelabra. There were also cheval glasses, or psyches, for seeing how one looked from hemline to coiffure; washstands; secretaires; tallboys or semainiers; lady's desks or bonheurs du jour; and chests of drawers. There were cabinets and cupboards and bookcases, and all of them, with a redesign based on classical themes, were drawn into the Empire fold.

The sofa table appeared in England first, in around 1800. Oblong, often with a drop leaf at each end, it took up residence in front of the sofa, where it was used for tea, or for doing one's sewing, or whatever. To discourage guests in the drawing room from congregating in a large circle, the English set about arranging their drawing-room furniture in scattered, more random-seeming groupings. As a result the backs of furniture, especially those of larger upholstered pieces, which had always been against a wall, now had to be made presentable.

Above: A double-pedestaled Biedermeier writing table provides a wonderful expanse for displaying the grain of wood veneer. Neoclassic tabletops were often supported by double columns as this one is.

Right: This three-legged fruit-wood table with a triangular base is a Biedermeier piece dating from about 1830. The urn on the table is also a Biedermeier piece made of burled wood. The sideboard is flame mahogany and was made in Copenhagen in 1911.

Left: These modern tea tables exhibit the marble tops typical of the Empire period. Their long legs and rectilinear shape are suited to a contemporary interior decorated in the neoclassic style.

Right: A marble-topped gueridon, this antique table's triangular base is ornamented with dolphins.

Right: This triangular table with steel-rod supports is a neat twist on the classic tripod table with metal legs. The table and matching vase were designed by Stephen Bumm.

Left: This newest of "neo" tables combines the essence of a classical tripod with the elegance of the gueridon. Three separate layers of glass are supported by a base with a rubberized finish. Called the AGIII table, it was designed by Al Glass.

Left: This small table with its network of metal supports provides an ideal surface for displaying ancient Mediterranean artifacts. Next to it is a carved Italian Empire chair.

Right: These little cigarette tables designed by Shelton Mindel & Associates have a neoclassic feel, exhibited by their tapering rectilinear legs. The tables are available in finishes of patinated-metal, marble, or pale-wood veneers.

CHAPTER
FOUR

NEOCLASSIC ACCENTS AND OBJECTS:
THE ORIGINALS AND THE UPDATES

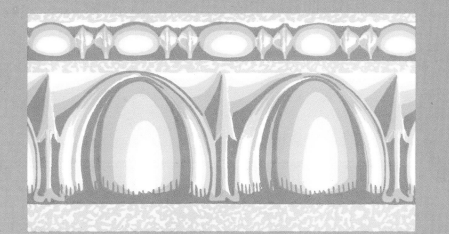

EMPIRE OBJECTS *Although Napoleon was perhaps first and foremost a man of war, he was also a man of politics. He felt it essential that other nations succumb not only to France's guns, but*

also to another sort of French weaponry: her culture. Keeping domestic industries afloat made good political sense, and having the rest of the Western world buy everything in France was a good way to keep local industry not only afloat but buoyant.

The style that Napoleon broadcast was his very own, and it was the decorative arts that drew his greatest energies. He was deeply involved with the design of many a product, and he was obsessive about quality. So, just as he had seen to it that the French silk industry was renowned for weaving the very best silks, he oversaw the output of other industries.

In the making of furniture, the French had dominated all competition because of their wizardry with metal — no matter how good they were with wood, no other country could produce such glorious furniture mounts. And what masterpieces the French craftsmen could produce for furniture, they could also produce for smaller decorative objects. The French excelled as well in the working of gold and silver, and in the forming and decorating of porcelain. All of these crafts created lovely embellishments for larger furnishings, but they were even more remarkable on their own. And because most decorative objects, from enormous chandeliers to tiny enameled boxes, are really nothing *but* ornament. here French prowess was most evident.

Of the Empire silversmiths, the two names heard most frequently are Martin-Guillaume Biennais and Jean-Baptiste-Claude Odiot. Biennais was by trade not a silversmith but an *ébéniste*, and among his earliest patrons were Napoleon and Josephine. The furniture he made was on a small scale — game and writing tables, and pieces called *nécessaires*, which were small cases fitted with toiletries, coffee-serving utensils, shaving kits, and the like. The case was made essentially of wood; it and its fittings, however, were sculpted and decorated, and included any number of materials, from silver gilt to porcelain and glass. By 1805, Biennais was Napoleon and Josephine's appointed silversmith, providing everything for them from tables to snuffboxes.

Odiot was a silversmith by trade, but he, like almost all of

Left: Beneath a Piranesi drawing of the ancient Greek Warwick vase is a somewhat smaller replica (the original is marble and weighs eight and a quarter tons). Beside it is a French clock of marble and bronze, capped by a bust of Benjamin Franklin, who was much admired by the French.

Right: The metal vases over the mantel were designed by Peter Coan of Red Roof Designs. Their stylized, contemporary feel manages to coexist nicely with ancient glass containers in an innovative mix in the neoclassic tradition.

Near right: A porcelain urn of the Empire period is flanked by an assortment of Napoleonic objects: On the right is a nineteenth-century metal inkwell in the shape of Napoleon's tomb, and on the left is a small statue of Napoleon himself.

Opposite: All of these contemporary vases are made of solid brass that has been patinated. Artist Monica Missio calls these particular Pompeii-inspired pieces CX. Their classic shapes and antiquated surfaces make these ideal objects for "new-neo" interiors.

his peers, collaborated with artists versed in other skills to produce some of the masterpieces of the period. Many of the silver pieces made by Biennais were from designs by Percier and Fontaine. Odiot, with the bronze founder Thomire, built a cradle designed by Prud'hon for Napoleon's son, the king of Rome, in 1811. It stands on cornucopia legs, its spindles linked by sculpted bees and its arched headboard capped with a Winged Victory holding a crown of laurel leaves and stars. A child would see the crown poised just above his head; a mantling eagle is perched at his feet. The cradle is, from stem to stern, silver gilt and mother of pearl, and was part of a suite of similarly opulent furniture for the infant king.

Both Odiot and Biennais also produced pieces that were entirely silver. As the Empire style took hold, these were to become, like all other decorative objects, more and more an excuse for sculptural tours de force. And so the chasing and etching of the pre-Napoleonic days gradually gave way to simple, classical forms with smoothly polished surfaces. But these surfaces were

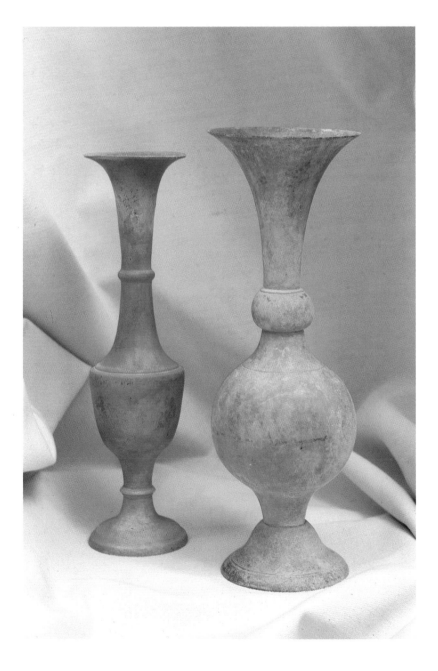

supported by, encircled by, and often nearly encased in the carved figures and motifs so beloved of Empire designers.

The Biedermeier tradition in decorative objects is far less opulent than the French Empire tradition, for many good reasons. One was that, in 1806, Emperor Franz Joseph I ordered all gold and silver objects to be turned over to the state, to be melted down. Austria was then at war with France, and this was an effort to alleviate the country's drastic financial situation.

And so, for items like candlesticks and jewelry, iron became a principal decorative metal. However, more candlesticks, and objects like small boxes, mantel clocks, and mirrors were made of the same pale wood veneers with ebonized (and more rarely, bronze) decoration as Biedermeier furniture. It was, until the defeat of Napoleon, a period of austerity, and the decorative arts largely reflected that. Even following the Congress of Vienna, a certain austerity persisted in much Biedermeier art.

Opposite: A contemporary bowl made of acid-etched glass with a base of patinated brass.

Left: Stephen Bumm designed this inverted-pyramid vase of Plexiglas with a steel-rod base. Though a far cry from Sèvres porcelain, its lines are dynamic and yet classic.

Right: A glowing collection of obelisks ranging from the eighteenth to the twentieth century. An ancient symbol of the Egyptians, the obelisk returned with Napoleon from his Egyptian campaign and became a signature of Empire.

Above: Architect Robert Stern designed this candlestick and salt and pepper shakers for Swid Powell. Attracted to the "beauty of the basic forms and profiles" of the classical, Stern designs objects with classical elements to, as he says, "extend the reach of my architectural ideas to the decorative."

CLOCKS

Mantel clocks were the perfect objects to endow with a miniature allegorical scene — they lived at eye level, chimed, and told time — all of which meant they were often and probably carefully looked upon. Their serious working parts were made by clock-masters — artists in their own right — and their cases were made by some of the master bronze founders, like Thomire, Feuchère, Ravrio, and Gallé. The French clocks were considered the best, and they were eagerly purchased elsewhere.

Muses, gods and goddesses, and ancient heros, in three dimensions and in bas relief, found themselves on what were really small sculptural masterpieces — which also happened to contain a clock. One clock has the muse Erato sculpted in patinated bronze. She stands on a gilt-bronze decorated marble base, dressed in flowing robes and playing a gilded lyre. It is in the middle of the lyre that one happens upon the clock face. Another clock shows Jason, in gilt bronze, reaching into a tree for the golden fleece. This time the clock face protrudes from the base of the tree, entangled in the folds of Jason's cloak and in the dragon that he has just slain. Fortune also makes her appearance on a clock, in a boat laden with wares — bounding over gilt-bronze waves.

Some clocks, instead of being small figural groups, were inspired by a Percier design for a clock in the form of a classical altar. Others looked like miniature porticos, flanked by columns. While they were made of any number of materials such as wood or marble, few clocks escaped the art of the bronze founder. His hand was to be seen everywhere — in their decorative mounts, column capitals and bases, miniature finials and feet; often even the dial and the pendulum were intricate masterpieces of bronze work. Porcelain was also used in the making of clocks — both as a material for decorative plaques and for entire clock cases.

Right: This small table clock is ornamented with classical urns but displays the simplified case shape and light-colored veneer that speaks of Austrian craftsmanship rather than French.

Left: Michael Graves's 1987 mantel clock designed for Alessi has the architectural look of many Biedermeier-era timepieces. Made of bird's-eye maple inlaid with ebonized wood, this clock boasts an eighteen-karat-gold pendulum.

ROMULUS, ROI DE ROME, ET TATIUS, ROI DES CURES.

Left: This gilded sculptural clock from the Empire period topped with a miniature astrolabe depicts the figure of Urania, the Greek muse of astronomy and celestial forces. Clocks were often a showcase for figures from mythology.

Above: This French clock, circa 1810, looks like a miniature portico flanked by columns. The other objects on the mantel are obelisks and copies of Greek oil lamps.

Right: Though this clock is from the French Empire period, it still keeps accurate time. The clock is ornamented with ormolu mounts. The dark-blue vase to its right is Berlin porcelain.

LIGHTING

Technologically, the end of the eighteenth century saw a very useful advance in the form of the improved oil lamp of a young Swiss inventor, Ami Argand. Although oil-burning lamps had been around since classical times, the new 1782 version burned brighter and cleaner than any of its predecessors. Still, as is so often the case, it took some time for technology to be completely integrated with fashion, and so the Argand lamp wasn't included in any of the inventories of Napoleon's palaces. Nor, for that matter, were any oil lamps, several new types of which were developed during Napoleon's reign.

But of candle-lit fixtures there was a plethora. There were chandeliers, lanterns, and wall brackets for walls and ceilings; and for floors and tables there were candlesticks, girandoles, and torchères. The inventories also listed the full gamut of other decorative objects, and, if cost is any indication of worth, they were as treasured then as they are now.

Comparing prices paid for furnishings in Napoleon's Grand Cabinet at Trianon, furnished in 1810, is a mini-education in what was considered valuable in his day. A group of two armchairs, twenty-four folding stools, two footstools, and a gilded-wood screen cost 6,784 francs, and 4,400 francs were paid for two cabinets of mahogany and gilt bronze with a one-inch-thick marble top. But the clockmaster Lepaute collected 4,000 francs for a single regulator clock, with a mahogany case and gilt-bronze mounts, and for an eighteen-light chandelier, the price was 5,200 francs.

If a chandelier or other light fixture was made of ormolu, chances are it was Parisian. Elsewhere, they were made of tôle, iron, blown glass and gilded wood, and plaster. Paint was often used as an embellishment for all of these, with or without gilding. The forms were as they had been during the Bourbon monarchy; only the motifs stamped them as Empire. Chandeliers generally consisted of a vase- or baluster-shaped central stem, encircled by light supports and hung with strings of crystal pendants. Any part of the stem and support system could be and generally was adorned with palmettes, acanthus leaves, lyres, masks, classical figures, and the like. Sconces were much the same, but instead of being curved and asymmetrical, they were linear and strictly balanced.

The lowly oil lamp, although it might not have ranked a position in one of the emperor's palaces, did appear elsewhere, and in some cases it was quite stylishly dressed. The painter Isabey had one atop an eight-foot-tall, fluted and paw-footed

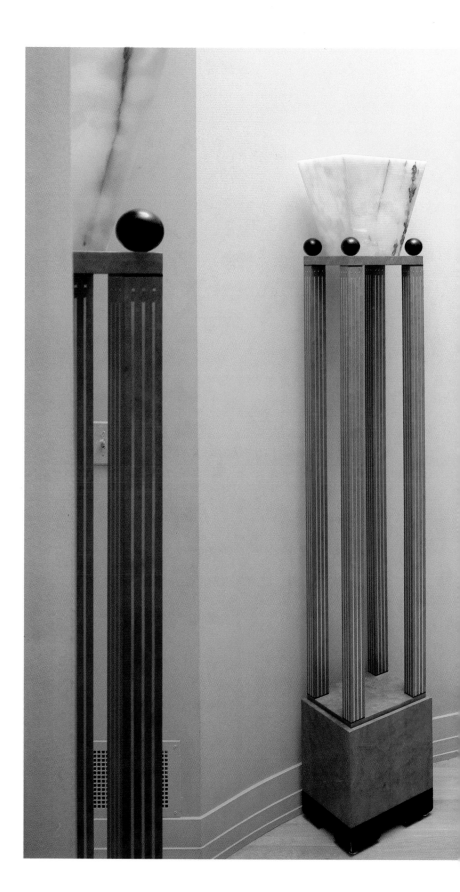

Left: These standing lamps designed by Michael Graves are a contemporary interpretation of the torchère, tall stands meant for the reception of candelabras and vases. The torchère was an important part of Empire-style design and remains an effective method for dramatic lighting of large spaces.

lampstand, the whole apparatus designed by Percier and Fontaine. Many of them could be mounted around a central support to form a chandelier, and with the advent at the turn of the century of the Carcel lamp, which allowed the oil reservoir to be beneath instead of above the flame, the designs became more similar to the familiar candle-lit chandelier. Even the emperor, although he may not have owned a lamp that actually burned oil, had a chandelier in his library that was designed to look like a classical oil lamp.

Right: These snake candlesticks look as though they might have served at Pompeii, though they are, in fact, turn-of-the-century pieces.

Right: An alabaster oil lamp of the Empire period hangs from the ceiling of this contemporary apartment. The small lamps on the mantel contribute to the neoclassic lighting effect with their fluted bases.

Right: These contemporary brass candlesticks acquired their antique patina through oxidization giving them an ancient Roman appearance.

Left: The base of this lamp designed by Michael Graves is wood treated to look like bronze. The lamp's design is derived from first- and second-century tripod-based lamps that were used in Roman military campaigns; they folded up so the troops could take them as they moved.

MIRRORS

Mirrors had also moved into the decorative forefront. As it had become possible to make larger and larger plates of glass, so, too, it had become possible to make larger mirrors, with the result that one could cover an entire wall, or even room, with mirrors. Their appropriateness, or lack thereof, was the subject of some discussion. Le Camus de Mezières, in his 1780 book *Le Génie de l'architecture*, said there ought to be intervals between mirror panels, for too much mirror produced "a sad and monotonous effect." Not heeding, or perhaps not having heard of, Le Camus' advice, a certain Mademoiselle Dervieux had her boudoir completely mirrored — walls and ceiling.

There were more decorative tricks to be played with large sheets of glass. Percier and Fontaine, in a room they designed in about 1801 for a Madame Moreau, placed a huge sheet of glass offering a view out into the garden behind and above a sofa, where it was customary to place a large mirror. The window was framed by a rectangular border containing sphinxes, urns, and medallions, just as a mirror would have been. The same device was used above fireplaces, requiring the flues to be somehow constructed around the sides of the glass. Despite this complicated construction, having windowed fireplaces became a popular fashion.

Opposite: This mirror depicts a classical frieze of a charioteer. In the neoclassic style, mirrors provided a decorative element, and their rectangular borders were often embellished with medallions and mythological figures.

Right: This gilded looking glass is American from the Federal period, as is the chandelier reflected in it. Atop the mahogany pier table is a whale-oil lamp from the first half of the nineteenth century. The curtains are arranged from a design in George Smith's Collection of Designs for Household Furniture and Interior Decoration, *published in London, 1808.*

Right: A large, gilded Italian neo-classic mirror sports a lion's mask, its mouth gripping a swag of laurel leaves. Its forepaws grip the top of the mirror, while the bottom of the mirror frame contains not only its hind legs but also its tail. Along the sides of the mirror coil a pair of serpents.

Right: This cheval mirror with a pedimented top is a Biedermeier piece crafted circa 1810. The chair is a design by Michael Graves.

CHINA

Porcelain factories of the Empire period reached an artistic level rivaled perhaps only by that of the bronze foundries. Technically, they had found a way of making vases over six feet high, their wares were gilded, their handles and details were elaborately sculpted, and their painters and other artisans were so highly skilled that the different European factories fought over them.

The porcelain pieces themselves also traveled, if not from factory to factory then certainly from country to country. The result was that in European porcelain design, perhaps more than in furniture design, there was a swifter exchange of ideas, and hence a more homogenous look to what was produced. There was also a fierce rivalry between manufacturers.

Still, at least for the duration of the Empire, the most remarkable pieces came out of the Sèvres factory. It was this factory which, just before the revolution, had succeeded in making vases of monumental size. They were in what was called the krater or Medici form, which looked something like a goblet with a very flared lip and an attenuated stem and foot, and they were liberally coated with bronze mounts. Although the factory apparently did not make any of the large vases after the Revolution, the form itself was often used. They also manufactured vases shaped like amphoras, and all of the forms that would come with a dinner service, from plates and bowls to cups and sauceboats.

Because much of the Sèvres factory's patronage came from the uppermost echelons of Empire society, much of the design was marvelously rich. Most of Napoleon's family were given kingdoms to oversee, and their porcelain all came from Sèvres. Anyone else who wished to be in the emperor's good graces followed suit. A service made for the queen of Bavaria is almost entirely gilded, with sprays and bands of brightly colored flowers, and, where needed, carved and gilded handles in the form of eagles' heads.

The typical Empire motifs, and the expected restrained classical forms, were well utilized by the porcelain manufacturers, and yet, as with the queen of Bavaria's service, sometimes motifs like colorful flower garlands, which would seem the antithesis of all that is Empire, appeared at the same time. For whatever the reason, such romantic motifs were tolerated and persisted, not only in France, but throughout Europe, carrying right into the much more highly florid Victorian era.

Still, the Empire motifs had the upper hand. Flowers or no, a piece of china with glaring eagle's head handles can scarcely

Below: The warmth of the wood finish of these beautiful Biedermeier pieces is complemented by the classical-looking pattern and rich colors of Graves's "Delos" china.

Left: A collection of Napoleonic Sèvres porcelain made for Versailles in the early nineteenth century mingles with classically gilded bookends and a bust of Napoleon.

be called sweet and romantic. The Musée des Arts Décoratifs in Paris has an album of designs from a company called Honoré et cie, covering the years 1796 to 1815. The engravings show such items as pots, clocks, inkwells, jardinières, and plates, and they are a compendium of Empire designs. There are paw-footed cups, scrolled handles ending in masks, carved lions' heads, acanthus leaves, and classical figures. The porcelain pieces are painted with allegorical scenes, classically styled cameo portraits, dolphins, lyres, and chimerae. The backgrounds of these porcelain pieces are the colors of neoclassicism like Pompeiian red, turquoise (like Egyptian faience) and different meticulously executed faux marbres.

These were designs for hard paste wares, which were fired first at a high temperature, then decorated and refired at a lower temperature. Hard paste ware was less expensive to make than fine porcelain, in part because much of the decorative work was done by artists in their own homes on a free-lance basis. But the quality of the work was high, quite possibly because Sèvres artists, who were allowed to do outside work, may have decorated many of the pieces.

Left: Bob Patino and Vicente Wolf designed this china with a classical feel. Likened to architectural drawings, it is called "Plate-O". The glasses and flatware were also designed by Patino and Wolf.

Below: This table setting unites the classic, the neoclassic, and the "new-neo." Two classical busts adorn the table set with "Corinth" pattern china designed by Michael Graves for Swid Powell.

WALLS

Ancient civilizations exercised a certain influence over the look of the whole neoclassic interior. Walls of the Empire period became works of art in their own right, chiefly at the hands of highly skilled painters, but also through the labors of wallpaper designers. The style was called *grotesque* in England, and depicted not at all what the name implies, but decorations derived from antique classical ruins found in excavations, or, to the Italians, *grottesci*. The English, notably Robert Adam, took up grotesque decoration with greater initial enthusiasm than the French, who referred to the style as *arabesque*. There was a stage when walls were painted to look as though the room was actually outside, with garden scenes and treillage, but this fashion gradually gave way to a more geometric, classical style as more documentation began coming from actual excavations.

Walls were decorated with medallions and rectangular panels, bordered with symmetrical scrollwork and the increasingly ubiquitous classical motifs. All of the decorations were either in bas-relief or painted to seem that way. Stenciling was also employed, usually to put a small, discreet, and sparsely spaced pattern on an otherwise plain wall, and to surround it with a heavy border. Soon these decorations were available in wallpaper — not only the patterns and murals for the main wall panels, but borders, friezes, and classical statues in niches. There was also paper that imitated draped silk. Any effect that could be painted was achieved by the wallpaper manufacturers; in fact, they even made paper to match fabric, so that an entire room could be decorated in a highly coordinated style.

Also incorporated into the decoration of walls was another painterly art; the simulation of various marbles, cut stone, and wood grains. The effect of these decorative arts was that interiors had less and less in the way of architectural ornament. Mantel pieces were reduced to simple chimney surrounds, and fireplaces were built into walls so that there was no protrusion. The carved pilasters, heavy cornices, overdoors, and the like from the first three-quarters of the century gave way to a more streamlined architectural box. While classical ornament was still very much in evidence, it was more commonly applied than intrinsic; however, this use of ornament was closer to that of interiors being uncovered in Pompeii than was the preceding style.

Atop their parquet floors, the emperor and his empress had, like French ruling families before them, Savonnerie carpets. They were tapestry woven, of strong colors, and generally had a large central rosette. And even if the rest of France and Europe

Above: This room, decorated by the firm of Lemeau and Llana, exhibits neoclassic decorative touches from the column to the moldings to the painted trompe l'oeil ceiling done by artist Michael Tyson-Murphy.

couldn't own a Savonnerie, they could certainly own, as many did, a Savonnerie-style carpet, woven in Brussels, Tournay, or Aubusson. The Aubusson factories also produced hand-knotted pile carpets. All of these carpets reflected neoclassic design influences, and although their colors were certainly Empire in their strength, for the most part the impression left by the carpet designs is not as dramatic as much of the rest of Empire design. This may have been because Percier and Fontaine never tried their hands at carpet design, and it may also have been just as well. Carpets that packed the same impact as the rest

of Empire design might have made rooms look more like battlefields than environments for living.

Machines had also been put to work making carpets, although the looms at this stage were still only mechanical, not steam powered. Nonetheless, both looped and cut pile carpets came off the mechanical looms. They could only be woven in small widths, then pieced together, so their patterns were necessarily small and repeated. Ironically, some of the makers of hand-produced carpets began to adopt the designs of the machine-made ones.

Opposite: A wall in this contemporary bedroom is covered with paper printed to emulate off-white draped silk — an undisguised reference to the draped fabrics that surrounded the beds of the Empire period and a common trick even in the Napoleonic era.

Left: The Deshon-Allyn House is full of decorative accents from the American Empire period, including authentic wallpaper and carpets in dining room and hall.

FABRICS

In the world of fabrics, the late eighteenth-century popularity of muslins and printed cottons had put the French silk industry into trouble. In response, Napoleon placed huge orders with the factories in Lyons. He and his decorators favored satins, both plain and with small repeated patterns, in colors such as golden yellow, bright green, and crimson. White was popular, too, which had to do with the association of classicism with purity and virtue. But, expectedly, this was far from the full range of colors in vogue at the time. Madame Recamier's *bateau en lit* had been surrounded with cascades of violet, buff, and black silks, and a bed upholstered for Napoleon by Darrac in 1809 was of a silk described as the color of citrus wood, decorated with stars of lilac, and with borders of silver brocade on a lilac ground. In about 1807, the Grand Cabinet of the emperor was hung in a color described as *tabac d'Espagne,* presumably a pale brown, with borders of blue and gold.

Curiously, although Napoleon's reputation is one of extravagance, most of what he spent was with the intent of reviving French industries. He reportedly was critical of Josephine's profligacy in her various redecorating schemes, and also evidently had strong words for his stepson Prince Eugene, who managed to spend more on the redecoration of his Paris house than he had in buying it. Still, the result of Napoleon's revivifying the silk industry was that his and many other French residences were draped in silk hangings — a fashion that spread, like all things French, throughout Europe.

The business of draping a room did not always stop at the cornice. Rooms were draped from top to bottom, with pleats converging in the middle of the ceiling to resemble tents. This style, which had been around before the Revolution, became hugely popular during the Empire period. Tent rooms, although they were at first the domain of men of military persuasions, also became the domain of women. Percier and Fontaine put together one for the boudoir of the Princesse de Courlande in 1802, having first tented the council chamber and vestibule at Malmaison with blue-and-white striped twill.

If the upholsterers of the period were worked overtime on wall and bed hangings, they were certainly given no rest when it came to window treatments. Function was not always a primary consideration; yardage, it would seem, was. The composition generally began with a pelmet, which was pleated or swagged, and might also be fringed or tasseled. They were often of two or more different brightly colored materials, with yet another

Opposite: This room, decorated by Lemeau and Llana, shows the dramatic effect of the neoclassic style of draping fabric. The double doors of the pedimented structure at the right open into a large closet that contains a bar and storage space.

Left: The drapes are a contemporary moiré silk, but the window treatment is an authentic neoclassic pattern. The fabric panels on the walls are a new striéd brocade damask from Rose Cumming.

reserved for the lining, which was designed to show. Beneath the pelmet hung the curtain, generally of muslin, and it, too, had its share of fringe. The treatment was often restrained with decorative tiebacks or brackets, and suspended from an array of poles, rods, rings, and finials. Furthermore, if a wall had more than one window, the treatment might run from one to the next in a continuous pattern.

Samples of silks and tapestries that were part of a commission begun in 1811 and finished just as Napoleon's empire was collapsing. The silks are currently stored in the Mobilier National, Paris. The pieces consist of panels ten feet high with a separate decorative border at the bottom.

Left: The abundance of French silk-taffeta curtains — draped and fringed much as they might have been specified by Percier and Fontaine — gives this room a forceful neoclassic profile.

Left: This "new-neo" interior by Richard Gillette is dramatically lit and draped in the spirit of neoclassic styles. The cotton gauze was pleated and treated with humidity to give it a diaphanous appearance.

CHAPTER
FIVE

IN THE NEOCLASSIC STYLE:
THE CONTEMPORARY HOME

RECENTLY REGENCY

Considering the flamboyance of the Empire style, and its propensity toward the grandiose, smart money would probably never have bet on its achieving much current popularity. But the style, or the style-makers, have fooled the pundits. Empire and its kin are popping up in every sort of interior, from period rooms replete with antiques all the way to contemporary rooms whose most aged furnishings still have wet paint, and yet whose inspiration is nearly two hundred years old.

David Easton's home is an example of the delightful result of the use of antique pieces in an appropriate setting that isn't quite "period." As recently as the early 1970s, good pieces of Regency furniture could still be purchased for a reasonable price. Those who, like Easton, appreciated the style while it was still considered merely old, now find themselves living with some old and very covetable pieces of furniture.

The first piece of Regency furniture Easton ever bought was a *klismos*-inspired chair painted to look like rosewood. Since then, he has accumulated an apartment full of Regency furniture and accessories.

Architecturally, the apartment seems to have little to do with the classical, or with the Regency. It is neither very large nor very grand. But it has been given, through a decorative sleight of hand, some of the distinction of a far grander space.

The neoclassic plays a major role in accomplishing this act. From the fine pieces of Regency furniture to the treatment of the windows, the decoration of this apartment owes a debt, albeit indirectly, to the ancient Greeks. Much of the furniture is Regency, the swags and jabots of the curtains and the striped wallpaper are typical of Regency designs, and many of the accessories, if not actually Regency themselves, are the sort of items one might have encountered in a house of the period.

Fine period furniture notwithstanding, David Easton's apartment is not in any way a reproduction of an early nineteenth-century English interior. It is hard to imagine a Regency living room with books stacked on the floor and on the back of the sofa, or with a basket full of logs by the fireplace. There is no doubt that this is an apartment that was designed to be lived in. It is, as Easton puts it, "a mix of period and comfortable."

Above: This apartment is chock full of charming neoclassic accents, from the Egyptian motif of the marble French Consulate–period mantel to the Regency-period terra-cotta bust depicting Janus, the Roman household god. His two faces symbolize age and youth, looking to the past and to the future.

Below: The rich red tone of the wallpaper gives warmth to this living room, which gets little natural light, while the stripes give an impression of height. The trim and dado are painted in faux marbre in a typically nineteenth-century fashion. The swags and jabots of the curtain treatment are also typical of the period.

Right: One of a pair of Sheraton-period painted Gainsborough chairs sits on the Bessarabian carpet. Next to it is the X-form Regency high-back chair that Easton calls a chauffeuse or fireside chair. These low, classically inspired seats make cozy resting places near the fire.

Left: The corner of the table displays its scagliola top depicting Greek vase figures. Scagliola is an ancient technique of mixing marble fragments into a compound that looks like marble. At left is a Regency cabinet with gilded sphinxes. In the center is the klismos-inspired chair that was the first piece in Easton's Regency collection.

EMPHATICALLY EMPIRE

Few would guess, on first looking at this room, that it was from the hand of a designer who had worked for two significant modernist architects, Marcel Breuer and Eero Saarinen. Saarinen designed both Dulles Airport in Washington, D.C., and the TWA terminal at New York's John F. Kennedy Airport, among other buildings, while the most familiar work of Breuer is his much-imitated 1928 chrome-plated tubular-steel chair. Both Breuer's chair and Saarinen's buildings are classics in their own right. Still, they, and modernism in general, seem an unlikely link to what Robert K. Lewis is up to in this room.

But the room may not be as far removed from the vision of the two modernists as it first appears. As Lewis says, "It is a contemporary room, but with a historical perspective." There is a modernist's sense of restraint here — cream walls, coir floor covering, and very minimal architectural detail. The room's spatial arrangement could also be said to derive from modernism. And that, in its own way, is strikingly Napoleonic. The painted wood *klismos*-style chairs are lined up along the wall, much as they might have been in any of the emperor's rooms. And the slipper chairs are placed squarely side by side. Jean-Antoine Houdon's sculpture of Lafayette is flanked by two windows; they in turn frame nineteenth-century iron jardinieres. The effect is one that Percier and Fontaine — and no doubt Breuer and Saarinen — would have applauded: clean, uncluttered, even bordering on rectilinear.

Lewis mentions another aspect to this room that keeps it from falling into the abyss of the period room: "I like to juxtapose a luxurious material, like the silk damask, with a simpler material, like the coir matting. Or the more elaborate treatment of the windows with the restrained treatment of the slipper chairs, which are really contemporary chairs." There is, however, plenty of historical reference in the detailing of the room. Lafayette's bust sits on a pedestal with distinct neoclassic overtones, right down to its painted marble finish. Hanging on the front of the pedestal is a miniature portrait by the Empire period French artist Saint Memin. It depicts Benjamin Harrison, the very man who commissioned Houdon, another French artist of the period, to make the bust of Lafayette as a gesture of thanks for his help during the Revolution.

So, from a modernist architectural background sprouts a de-

signer whose rooms have a traditional bent. As Lewis says, "We are all products of our time. And our work is a product of our interests. I can't say I wasn't profoundly influenced by modernism, but lately I've become very interested in the Jeffersonian period. This room pays homage to that period."

Left: Windows elaborately draped in silk frame nineteenth-century jardinieres. Houdon's bust of Lafayette is symbolic of the French influence on American interiors of the period.

Right: Painted-wood klismos-style chairs line one wall of this decorative homage to the Jeffersonian period in America. The framed architectural prints testify to designer Lewis's interest in the classical.

DISCREET ANTIQUES

It should be said that the terms *traditional* and *contemporary*, which are firmly entrenched in the design lexicon, are about as loose as definitions can be. The line that separates the two is fuzzy at best and confounds any attempt to clarify it. Dealing with a style as filled with historic reference as the neoclassic doesn't do much to make definitions any simpler.

In the end, however, it is unlikely that a serious dispute would ever arise over which category a project falls into. Categories are a useful point of departure for discussion, but inevitably a discussion is about whether or not a room is any good, and why.

Asked about his design objective, Gary Hager's response always revolves around tranquility — an adjective that hardly springs to mind when one contemplates the neoclassic. But Hager explains, "I choose the furniture that doesn't have the gilded bronze and carving." So the furniture he uses "is really very restrained. It is rich without being embellished, and I think rather honest." And so, consequently, are the rooms he designs.

This room does not boast an excess of architectural ornament or any single feature, such as an elaborate mantelpiece or window grouping, that commands attention. It has been up to the designer to make what he would of the space. Hager rearranged walls and doorways to make the rooms "as orderly as possible, so they would work with furniture that is so architectural."

"I try not to be influenced by fashion," Hager says. "It happens that I love antiques and clean simple lines. They are timeless, and I'm not one who believes in redecorating every time a new fashion blows through."

Left: Hager gives the antique a contemporary touch in the living room. The antique Regency table, Louis Philippe open armchair, and French Consulate bergère (found in the basement of a previous apartment), are complemented by the reproduction Directoire chairs in painted and sandblasted oak.

Below: In the bedroom, are a pair of X-form benches. Here, as elsewhere in the apartment, there is a mixture of periods that comes all the way up to the present.

Left: The dark green glazed wallpaper of the hallway gives the paler-colored living room beyond a look of neoclassic serenity. With its wood floors and somewhat bare walls, the apartment avoids a cluttered look. As Hager points out,"There is no chintz in the apartment."

DECO ECHO

Just as there are plenty of variables that flag a room as traditional, there are those that are unmistakable banners of contemporary design. So — even in a room full of antiques — track lighting, clean, unadorned walls, and a lacquered Parson's table are sending a clear message. In a contemporary setting, objects find themselves serving functions for which they weren't originally designed — column capitals as table supports, for example, or quilted movers' blankets as upholstery. Contemporary design is all about probing new ideas, and its joy is that anything goes.

If some neoclassic furniture can be accused of being overexuberant, then a contemporary setting can be used to rope it in. And, in an age when contemporary design might be said to have attained the pinnacle of sobriety, a chair or two adorned with carved and gilded sphinxes will certainly ease the atmosphere. It can be played both ways.

It may seem as though the solutions for particular projects land in the laps of architects or designers whenever they need it, but most of them will confess that there is always something about the space itself that inspires them and sets the course for the project. For Ronald Bricke, a designer who is a confessed admirer of the neoclassic, the approach to an apartment with a very powerful sense of symmetry was an easy call. It begged for furnishings that were equally symmetrical. For Bricke, that meant not only nineteenth-century versions of the neoclassic (Empire and its peers), but also Art Deco. The two are much alike, he finds, being "either extremely simple and architectural, or very decorative. Plus, in both there is an overriding sense of the classical."

Bricke adds that for him, there are two ways that neoclassic styles can be handled. "Because the shapes and sizes are so powerful," he says, "you can either give them a lot of space, so they stand on their own, or you can enclose them in a cocoon of opulence, so they became absorbed into the background." For this apartment, with its tall ceilings, strong central axes, and spaciousness, he opted for the former.

The furniture forms make all the statements in this apartment. That is not to give the impression that the rooms are filled with a collection of strong furniture designs, all vying for attention. There is cohesion in the room's symmetry and in the similarity of the furniture's forms and veneers.

Left: Despite the exotic accent of leopard skin, the room is restrained — cream with white trim for the walls, cream for most of the upholstery. And although the carpet is a rich green, it doesn't compete with the furniture.

Below: A pair of Biedermeier armchairs flank a double-pedestaled desk of similar origins and similarly richly patterned wood. The pair of gilt-bronze lamps and objects on the table complete the symmetrical setup. Above is a nineteenth-century Austrian clock on a bracket.

Right: An Art Deco bar stands isolated to one side, but it is balanced by a marble-topped nineteenth-century table. The mirror and wall brackets complete the sense of symmetry.

Opposite: In the bedroom a small vase-shaped Biedermeier dressing table stands on its own like a piece of sculpture.

SWAN SONG

In this apartment the use of neoclassicism is referential, for, in fact, there are few classical motifs, and even those are interpretive rather than exact. As with so many a New York City apartment, the major shortcoming with this one was its small size. If that is no longer immediately apparent, it is thanks to the ingenuity of both the architects and the designer.

The first work that was done to this apartment was to pull it — nearly completely — down. "Basically," says designer Victoria Borus, "everything, inside and out, is new." What is now the balustrade around the terrace was once a stucco wall, and it was the classical feel of the balustrade that launched the mood of the rest of the apartment.

"Apart from the columns, one of which is structural, there is nothing strictly classical about the background of the apartment," says Borus. "But the flow of space is very formal, or axial, which I think is what gives the impression of classicism." And, as anyone in the design business will tell you, once you get the structure, or "the bones" of a space right, the rest will fall into place.

Which is why an apartment can house, as this one does, some icons of modernity — carpeted platform, bare cream-colored walls, a pharmacy lamp — alongside the demure gilded settee and chairs from 1920s France, ancient vases from Jerusalem, and nineteenth-century French dining chairs. And, as Borus says, the success of the apartment is due to the fact that "it is so small — tiny, really. But it still has a sense of grandeur."

Left: The columns give a classical feel to this apartment designed by Victoria Borus in collaboration with Red Roof Designs. The dropped picture molding rings around the columns and the moldings at the top of the baseboard and elsewhere are based on the V-shaped molding of the window mullions.

Below: In a mix of cultures, a nineteenth-century Japanese silk obi adorns the dining table, while pencils covered with Italian marbled paper provide an ornamental touch. Obelisks, classical silver candlesticks, and nineteenth-century French fauteuils lend an Empire flavor to the setting. Swans' heads are typical of Empire design and are also a favorite motif of the client.

Left: The bathroom fixtures with swan's-head faucet and handles were custommade. They match the other hardware throughout the apartment (door levers, window levers, and so forth).

Right: On the terrace, the swans' heads that are visible are the backs of nineteenth-century Italian folding garden furniture. The teacup is from a 1950s Tiffany design called "Black Victoria." The towels are French.

CLASSIC SYMMETRY

The house of Michael La Rocca does not boast high ceilings, baseboards, cornices, or paneling. Nor would it ever occur to La Rocca to attempt putting in such details. "It would be a terrible disservice to the house," he feels, "something like putting a short fat woman in a full-length gold brocade gown."

"The outside of the house," he continues, "is a very basic, simple form in glass and cedar, and it is surrounded by a wood of fifty-foot white pines." Based on that description, one would think that his inspiration for treating the interior would be from Oregon, Maine, or even Scandinavia. His travels to the ancient towns of Italy, however, were what inspired him.

"In towns like Florence, you see what look like the plainest, most humble buildings. But step inside the gates and you're in a totally different world. That was what I wanted here. It's a simple house, but when you come inside you are presented with something totally unexpected." Which is true, for inside is a collection of extraordinary neoclassic furniture.

And yet again, it is a strong sense of symmetry that lets the house work, something that La Rocca created from the outset. The living room, which he added to the house, is centered on an axis, from main doorway to fireplace. All the other architectural elements — tall glass doorways, bookcases, and windows — are either on or are perpendicular to that axis, and they are all the same height. So the room has an almost templelike regimentation to it.

Furniture arrangement follows suit. It emphasizes the room's axes and is almost uniformly squared off. The only deviations are two large, overstuffed armchairs, which are set at angles to flank the fireplace, each anchoring its own corner of a decidedly square composition. The whole furniture group sits on a floor of square leather floor tiles — arranged in large rectangular panels — bordered in bleached pine.

The result, while it sounds stiff and proper, is restful, and allows La Rocca to get away with a rich mix of furniture. "It is," as he points out, "a fairly catholic approach to design. I filled the house with the things that I enjoy living with, so it's a decided mixture of periods and styles." And while, as usual, it is the Empire group that displays the most bravado, the house carries the mix off well, fulfilling the designer's intention of creating a sense of surprise.

Above: An Italian Empire chair has carved and gilded details and is upholstered in a bold flowered tapestry. The elaborately carved console table — thought to be Irish — and the carved and gilded sunburst, inset with a mirror, are part of the rich mix of periods and styles.

Below: In the dining room an interesting neoclassic blend is achieved as a Roman bust and a sculptural group of fluted columns complement a set of Biedermeier chairs.

ESSENTIAL EMPIRE

When Bob Patino and Vicente Wolf use Empire pieces in their designs, they handle them as a careful chef would rich ingredients, sprinkling them sparingly. The designers feel that such an approach is important to appreciating the style. Patino and Wolf's strategy is to use a clean, spare, modern environment in which antiques appear here and there. This way, they say, the pieces do not overwhelm and their individuality is allowed to show. Patino and Wolf feel that the use of the period room in this country is somewhat artificial — that contemporary design is really what the American lifestyle is all about — and that the most natural place for pieces from other periods to live is within a contemporary design.

Everything about this oceanfront house allows the fine period pieces it contains to stand out and be recognized. The intentional contrast between Empire and everything else begins with a crude, crabbed orchard stone floor that was irregularly laid, and continues with white walls and ceilings made flawlessly smooth with spray lacquering. In between, the furnishings are often sleekly contemporary, punctuated by Empire pieces, which call attention to themselves because they are so unexpected.

Like important pieces of sculpture that are given space to be shown off, the columns at the entrance to the sitting room are highly visible against the blank walls and white furnishings. The chair behind the columns has Empire echoes in its white cloth covering, although the treatment for an Empire chair would have been far more luxurious. The traditional use of a contemporary mirror at the back of the room brings the ocean indoors with its large and splendid reflection.

In their spare designs, Patino and Wolf pay great homage to the Empire style, highlighting its specialness and, more importantly, our contemporary need and desire for its influences.

Above: The elegant bathroom is dominated by a French eighteenth-century copper bathtub. The oversize bath towels covering the chair recall the draping effects of neoclassicism, and the sphinx adds an amusing Napoleonic touch.

CHAPTER
SIX

THE NEW NEO

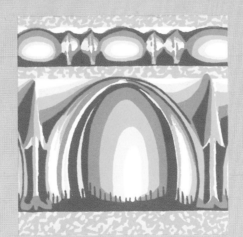

ROMAN ROMANCE

As Tom Fox and Joe Nahem aptly display in the interior they designed for this house, the wonder of the classical is that it can fit in with any style and, while retaining its own strong character, elevate and add sophistication to that style. Here there is a definite romanticism, an opulence that is refined by the introduction of classical lines and forms.

Designers Fox and Nahem gutted the inside of this 1920s house and rebuilt it. The living room is lined with classical architectural materials: the walls have been frescoed and sealed with beeswax to achieve an overall patina, the floors are slabs of French limestone. In addition to these classical elements, however, the room is draped with an aura of romance.

The sofa, an update of a piece from earlier in the century, is a poetic curve that sets off the other romantic elements, from the French damask covering of a chair designed by Fox and Nahem to the Impressionist painting on the wall behind it. Sitting amid the more rational lines of neoclassic pieces, these emotional forms bring out the softer side of neoclassicism. Hence, the fanciful curves of the antique tripod garden tables are accentuated. The original Robert Adam urns from the late eighteenth century, covered with moss and terra-cotta draping, also show a more sweeping side to neoclassicism.

Fox and Nahem take advantage, however, of the straight edges of classicism by designing very clean-lined pieces, the best example of which is perhaps the chest in the living room. Constructed of sandblasted steel and topped with a classical "roof," the piece incorporates the grid pattern that is found throughout the house and ends in silver-leaf pads that echo the supports of the French Consulate chairs found in the living and dining rooms. Contemporary and practical (inside is stereo equipment for which the chest was specially designed), the chest beautifully accommodates Regency mirrors, old opaline glass lamps, and an antique Sheffield sterling tray.

Fox and Nahem say that they like to use classical elements in their work because they take the edge off the newness of today's designs. This house certainly goes a long way toward proving that statement.

Left: The bathroom displays the other side of the crossed squares and classical eaves of the fresco piece used in the bedroom. Aside from the French limestone of the counter, the fixtures are sleekly contemporary.

Above: In the dining room, the French Consulate chairs, representing a brief period between the Directoire and Empire styles, surround a table topped with French limestone. The chandelier of hand-blown glass is a new piece designed by Fox and Nahem. Together the furnishings make a boldly classical statement within the contemporary walls of the room.

Left: In the bedroom, the designers emphasize the monumentality of classicism with this dramatic fresco piece. Reaching toward fourteen-foot ceilings, the piece brings the architectural indoors in more than a symbolic sense.

Right: The crossed squares that frame the entrance to the dining room continue the classical grid pattern and use the geometrics of classicism in a brightly contemporary manner. The steellike appearance of the squares was created with the use of metallic car lacquer.

Left: The antique tripod garden tables in front of the sofa are French Empire-style pieces made of gunmetal. They are a perfect match for the French Consulate chair at the left. With its tapered back legs, straight back, and front legs supported by metal balls, the chair is quintessentially neoclassical.

FOUND CLASSICISM

Designer Michael Kreiger's apartment and workspace is ordered with all the symmetry, formality, and strong lines of classicism. That this is achieved with often radical contemporary contributions is delightfully disconcerting. The harmony that results is a testament to the resiliency of classicism, but also to the importance of finding elements common to both periods.

What Kreiger found was a reliance on the use of geometries and a recognition of the importance of metal. Straight lines and basic shapes, cornerstones of classicism, have been revived in contemporary use, with the notable addition of the circle, which was not standard in classical or neoclassic interiors. As a rejection of the modernist cube, the circle is a hallmark of Postmodernism that mingles nicely with the more angular forms of classicism. As for metals, because of their rarity, they were the focus in

any classical or neoclassic piece that used them. In a post-industrial era, metals are important for the opposite reason—because we are used to having them all around us. In this apartment, the link between the old and the new views on metal is made in a beautifully elegant way.

Metals are everywhere, particularly in the use of found objects. In the bedroom, a shock absorber from a truck and a mahogany bowling ball grace the chest, while an air-conditioner grille mounted on a black field by Kreiger becomes a work of art for the room. The wrought-iron and gold leaf-gilded bed frame, made in Paris in the 1940s, complements the metals and the geometries of the room. Elsewhere, an Empire-style tripod table is set with old gateposts placed like precious antiquities, while next to it, a metal and weathered-leather chair designed by sculptor Alberto Giacometti contributes a classic, timeless feel. Above this scene, a face looks out from a frieze that was retrieved from a torn-down building in the Bronx.

A theatrical tour de force that is calmed by the lines of classicism, this apartment showcases the ability of the designer to combine the patently traditional with the wildly untraditional by respecting like forms and materials.

Above and preceding page: In the bedroom, the juxtaposed circles and straight lines enhance one another in a disarming fashion. From the Greek key figure on the screen designed by Kreiger to the circles on the bed frame and chest, to the triple symmetry of the rice-paper lamp, ancient and modern shapes and symbols create a dynamic classicism.

Right: A reproduction of an actual 1930s design, this table has a neo-classic look. The supports that hold its marble surface are in the classic Greek key design. The metal base and legs of the table were originally painted, but Kreiger stripped the paint in a process that allows the metal to oxidize over the years.

Right: Antique Regency hall chairs, embellished with a crest of an arm and fist, correspond to the overall design with geometries of their own. An overtly classical — almost comically so — zinc finial salvaged from a Parisian building presides between the two chairs.

GRAND ILLUSIONS

When Richard Gillette designed this apartment in a magnificent prewar building, he sought out the glamour of classicism — and found it. He wanted to bring the classical facade of the building indoors and recreate for the apartment the grandeur that exists on the outside. To do this, painter and designer Gillette relied heavily on the historic technique of painting faux finishes that is becoming increasingly popular today.

Although the practice of painting illusions of certain materials to fool the viewer is an ancient one, one reason it is being revived in contemporary design has to do with its practicality. Today, installing the rich marbles and stones that faux finishes imitate is often difficult or even impossible because of the pro-

hibitive cost or unavailablity of such materials; sometimes their very weight presents structural problems. Painted faux finishes, then, provide the kind of balance that is important in contemporary design: artistry combined with usefulness.

The use of classical influences also solved a problem for Gillette. He knew that the airy openness of a classical treatment would make this small studio apartment appear larger.

The walls certainly set the stage for something classical to happen. A magnificent imitation of sandstone, they are made even more convincing with the faux moss in the nooks and cracks — another example of the advantage of using paint over the real thing. In the dining area, the reclining forms of classicism are used to create — or recreate — a simple glamour.

The linen on the seats of the banquettes furthers the sense of the classical, and the modern glass of the table does not detract from that mood, but serves instead to create a little intrigue. There are a variety of influences from many different periods here, but because the outlines of the space are classical, everything works together. The formality pulls it all into place.

Preceding page: To make the banquettes and surrounding shelves, Gillette distressed wood with a hammer and plane to create the chips and imperfections of stone, and then painted it to look like granite. To the left is a real Greek vase on a real marble column, making it a puzzle for the viewer to determine what in the room is real and what is fake.

Above: In the dining area, the leopard stools are topped with metal interpretations of the Empire scroll.

Left: A sense of urban primitivism prevails in the living/sleeping area. The metal 1930s chairs bear the sloping arms of the Empire style, but the arms are made of chains. The tripod table with its marble surface and hoofed feet is an antique from the Empire period.

DIVAN RIGHT

If there is one element that all architects and designers will stress about their work, it is the matter of appropriateness. From the limitless assortment of design references available to them, it is their job to select what is appropriate for a particular project. Into the equation go the space, its uses, and, of course, the needs and tastes of the client. Designer Peter Carlson had the additional problem of clients who had completely divergent points of view — she wanted a period look, he wanted modern.

The solution was a balancing act. Carlson gutted a space in a postwar building in New York and gave it a large entrance gallery with a stone floor, accessed by pairs of doors. "The apartment," he says, "began to have a strong sense of updated classicism — a simplicity of line and strength of form." Leaving out the characteristic heavy moldings and other signature details, Carlson captured the essence of the classical proportion.

Left: The "Salona" sofa was designed by Carlson specifically for this apartment. Carlson, who has long been fascinated by Empire designs, wanted to design something in steel, and he also wanted to design a piece with a frieze. The sofa presented him with an opportunity to do both. The two thin cushions were inspired by a photo of furniture in Pauline Rothschild's apartment in Paris. The desk in the foreground, also designed by Carlson, is made of rift oak, with pickled panels outlined by angled moldings and rectilinear faux ivory knobs. To help out what he refers to as "a distinctly uninteresting window," Carlson made curtains of diamonds of glazed silk.

Left: The classical shape of the gilded mirror and the graceful lines of the sofa transform the room into an Empire-style salon. The iridescence of the steel is heightened by the fabric of the cushions and the elegantly patterned pillows.

Right: The living room is a consummate mix of the contemporary and the classical. The vitrines designed by Saladino that sit side by side against the wall are each hinged in the middle. Because the outside doors of the pieces are flat, the columns are only reflected in the mirrors at their backs.

136 IN THE NEOCLASSIC STYLE

GOOD BONES

"The system of classical orders and attending vocabulary of classic architecture is a wonderful skeleton, and I always go back to good bones." This is how designer John Saladino describes the importance of classical influences in his work, influences that go far beyond the surface. In this duplex, the use of the classical is so pervasive, so ingrained in the philosophy of the space that the owners don't just live *with* the classical, they live *within* it.

The apartment has a Roman layout. The long foyer is meant to convey the feeling of an outdoor piazza, and the rooms that open off it represent little buildings that one enters to be "indoors." The architectural materials used in the foyer give the effect of being in the street: fragments of giant columns, rough plaster, and ruined stone. As one enters each of the rooms that

run parallel to the foyer — the living room, dining room, and kitchen — one gets the sense of entering refined spaces of separate structures that are finely and luxuriously finished.

Saladino compares the effect to a shell; the outside is crude and hard, the inside smooth and delicate. Another way to look at it is through the layers of classicism. The outside uses ancient Roman classicism; it is physical and architectural, strict and cold like the stone that was used to build it. Inside, however, is the neoclassic, focused on creating atmosphere, refinement, and softness — warm, like the woods used in its furnishings.

The jewellike living room is opulent yet comfortable. With its furniture arranged in "pockets," it is like a piazza with clusters of conversationalists; a very human element is brought to the house. The use of mirrors, columns, white accents, cool metallic colors, and wood give the blend of antiquity and modernity that is the essence of the neoclassic style. Certainly if the bones are good, then what Saladino used to flesh them out makes a grand whole in this stunning apartment.

Left: Crude plaster and urns are placed against the walls above the stairs. The rails of the romantically curved stairway look like metal interpretations of the draped fabrics of Empire.

Below: The second-floor bedroom, with its metallic columns and furnishings and elegant fabrics, is another rich shelter for the inhabitant — a mix of today and a more luxurious time.

Above: A cornice wraps around the living room, bearing contemporary stylized designs of columns in an almost staccato pacing. The fireplace below echoes the design.

Right: In the living room, antique Regency chairs and Empire tables fit comfortably among Saldino's contemporary sofa and chair designs. The white armchairs are period pieces that have been slipcovered.

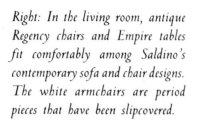

Left: The dining room speaks more of French elegance than opulence. The ceiling is painted with an enlarged version of a pattern taken from the fabric on the walls. The sideboard designed by Saladino uses contemporary elements while lightly borrowing from the classical.

WHITE DESIGN

For this apartment in a newly constructed building, designer Michael de Santis took the neoclassic style and clothed it in white. The apartment is relatively small, so de Santis felt a light and airy approach was needed to open up the space. And since white has neoclassic associations, emphasizing the connection between classicism and purity, the choice was a natural one for a design that combines the best of formal neoclassic elements with the best of contemporary simplicity.

The deft blend of classic and contemporary begins in the den. Here, a clean-lined but luxurious sofa designed by de Santis strikes a purely modern note. A trompe l'oeil painting and a modern glass wall coexist beautifully. In the dining area and living room, the commanding air of classicism is extended to a larger space. The flooring is white marble; columns and raised

Left: In the living room, with its contemporary furnishings, the classical mood is sustained by the symmetry of the lamps and the slipper chairs with their identical blue-and-white silk pillows. The classical forms of the obelisk, table, and chair contribute to the overall look.

Right: The mirrors make the apartment appear larger and, by visually multiplying the columns, add to the grandeur. The dining room chairs borrow from the basic Empire form with their fluted "Greek" back legs that get progressively smaller toward the feet. The contemporary use of upholstery completely hides any wood, even on the legs.

baseboards were installed on the bare walls and finished in the refined lines of Empire. The pineapple sculptures on the sleek modern table designed by de Santis put the neoclassic influence firmly in place with their traditional bases and their double symmetry when reflected in the mirror.

The classic and the contemporary are such a perfect pair because of the simplicity and purifying elements that are basic to each. Just as the decorative elements on the reproduction Empire chair in the living room do not interfere with the refined form of the piece, so it is with the apartment as a whole: The contemporary never clutters or confuses the classical lines that are so strong throughout the space, but instead adds intrigue.

Right: The classical landscape on the wall in the den is actually a painting on matchstick blinds. The trompe l'oeil artistry creates a sense of other palaces off in the distance.

NEO ORDER

"There is," as Lee Mindel of Shelton Mindel & Associates says, "no recipe for achieving a look. The decisions we make are not arbitrary: there is a reason behind them." For an apartment in a building that he describes as "an eclectic 1920s version of the late eighteenth century — or the *My Fair Lady* version of the original thing," the firm's response was, for the rooms themselves, "a modernist's approach, with overlapping and layering of space." And for furnishings, "to refer to what we saw in the style of the building."

That, for the most part, is the neoclassic. The appeal of neoclassic furnishings, Mindel points out, is that they are based on architecture, and that they present a sense of order. And order is what this apartment is all about. From the trail of urns that leads you from the front hall, through the living room,

Opposite: The striations on the silk covering the chairs imitate the black pen-and-ink lines on the contemporary screen behind them. The architectural images on the screen represent the overall approach to the room — classical order within overlapping space.

Left: This view from the dining area shows the careful placement of urns and other classical objects throughout the space, which has the effect of leading one through the living room and up to the study.

Right: The grid-shaped wall paneling in the dining area conceals storage, with one colored panel lending a refreshing irregularity to the design. Another irregular element is the beam which, by hanging over the dining room, makes the living room appear bigger than it is.

Opposite: The grid-shaped balcony surrounds echo the paneling and parquetry in the dining area and also the grid of the windowpanes that dominate the living room.

and up into the study, everything — or almost everything — in the apartment is about order.

The collection of bookends in the living room all have classical architectural themes. The ceiling is surrounded by a border of acanthus leaves, and its center sports an alabaster oil lamp that could be right out of Herculaneum. The round end table and the little cigarette tables that the firm designed also have a neoclassic feel. A Jacob brothers bergère and a Thomas Hope chair add authentic neoclassic touches to the rational, orderly, yet warm and livable space.

BACK TO BIEDERMEIER

Architect and designer Michael Graves often brings the significance of classical influences to the attention of the contemporary world with his buildings, interiors, furniture, and objects. What is important to Graves about the use of the classical element in interiors is its humanism. The form and height of classical pieces within a house, he says, correspond to the human scale and identity in a way never intended by the creations of modernism.

The Keystone House, which Graves designed inside and out, is a rich journey through the realm of the familiar made somewhat unfamiliar through new compositions. This is the result of Graves's use of classical references in heartily contemporary designs. Here he turns to the particular neoclassic influence of Biedermeier, with its light woods and contrasting dark accents, its pared-down forms and elegant lines, to create his own design stamp.

In this house, the *presence* of the classical is always there, even when the expression is very contemporary. It is a classical progression to place the living room adjacent to the dining room, and the kitchen on the other side of that, in a symbolic and practical recognition of the residents of the house — that they will need the convenience of one particular room opening out to another. A chair rail runs around the walls in the entry to the dining room and is accentuated by the use of different colors above and below it. For Graves, such a treatment is a symbolic way of dividing up space the way a person experiences it in nature. The chair rail acts as a horizon line within the room, promoting the idea that the area below it signifies the base or ground, and that above relates to the void of space beyond, all of which reflects the size and scale of the person within the space. With classical references such as these, Graves is helping to revive a concern for people having a relationship to the space within which they live.

Other features take into account the needs of the people who use the space and its furnishings. The simple form of the dining room chairs, for example, is graced with detailing that serves a practical, as well as decorative, purpose. The Biedermeier scroll at the top provides a handhold when pulling a chair out from the table, and a cutout at the back, although symbolically resembling an entrance to an Egyptian temple, perhaps, provides

practical comfort to anyone who sits in the chair. The leather seat is a smooth reintroduction of contemporary sensibilities. All in all, Graves has designed a house that is provocative in its contemporary expressions, comforting in its classical ones, and fascinating when the two mingle.

Left: With the torchères in the rotunda outside the living room, the classical is immediately evoked. The torchères act as columns to herald the entrance to the room. Their rectilinear bases recall the lines of Empire and Biedermeier. They also serve the practical purpose of getting the light up to the height appropriate for the space.

Above: Column imagery is echoed on either side of the massive marble fireplace in a streamlined contemporary interpretation. The settees are Graves's own intriguing mix of Biedermeier and contemporary elements.

Left: Graves had the standard German nineteenth-century kitchen in mind when designing this one, a hygenic white space that, above all, speaks of order. The small black square tiles are classical in their pacing, contemporary in their lines.

Above: The dining table and chairs designed by Graves make graceful use of Biedermeier elements. The pale wood of the bird's-eye maple gets slightly darker and warmer with age. The Biedermeier tendency to contrast light with ebony tones is seen here in the rings around the legs, which form stylized columns when paired with the classical base.

Above: This chair, designed by Graves for Sunar, is upholstered in leather. Like the settees in the living room, the scrolled arms, tapered legs, and wood veneers of Biedermeier are set amid the more luxurious shape and upholstered look of today.

SOURCES

Note: Many of these show-rooms are for the use of dealers, decorators, architects, or designers and are not retail outlets open to the public. Please call for information first.

ANTIQUES

DIDIER AARON
32 East 67th Street
New York, NY 10021
(212) 998-5248

AGOSTINO ANTIQUES, LTD.
808 Broadway
New York, NY 10003
(212) 533-3355
(212) 533-5566

A LA VIELLE RUSSIE
781 Fifth Avenue
New York, NY 10022
(212) 752-1727

YALE R. BURGE
305 East 63rd Street
New York, NY 10021
(212) 838-4005

ELIZABETH R. DANIEL
2 Gooseneck Road
Chapel Hill, NC 27514
(919) 968-3041

DAVID DUNTON ANTIQUES
Route 132 off Route 47
Woodbury, CT 06798
(203) 263-5355

FLORIAN PAPP INC.
962 Madison Avenue
New York, NY 10021
(212) 228-6770

LE CADET DE GASCOGNE
Gilbert Gestas, Inc.
1015 Lexington Avenue
New York, NY 10021
(212) 744-5925

CLINTON R. HOWELL
Westchester Avenue
Scotts Corners
Poundridge, NY 10576
(914) 764-5168

JACOB FRERES LTD.
1018 Madison Avenue
New York, NY 10021
(212) 249-7622

KIRK-BRUMMEL ASSOCIATES
979 Third Avenue
New York, NY 10022
(212) 477-8590

H.M. LUTHER, INC.
999 Madison Avenue
New York, NY 10021
(212) 439-7919

MACY'S INTERIOR DESIGN STUDIO
The Corner Shop
34th Street & Broadway
Ninth Floor
New York, NY 10001
(212) 736-5151

MALMAISON
29 East 10th Street
New York, NY 10003
(212) 473-0373

METROPOLITAN MUSEUM OF ART
82nd Street & Fifth Avenue
New York, NY 10028
(212) 879-5500

MUSEUM OF FINE ARTS
465 Huntington Avenue
Boston, MA 02115
(617) 267-9300

REYMER-JOURDAN
45 East 10th Street
New York, NY 10003
(212) 674-4470

RITTER ANTIK INC.
1166 Second Avenue at 61st Street
New York, NY 10021
(212) 644-7442

TOTO ROUSSEAU
125 East 57th Street
First Level
New York, NY 10022
(212) 751-7008

NIALL SMITH
344 Bleeker Street
New York, NY 10012
(212) 255-0660

VICTOR ANTIQUES
135 Sullivan Street
New York, NY 10012
(212) 995-9491

FREDERICK P. VICTORIA
154 East 55th Street
New York, NY 10022
(212) 755-2549

ANGUS WILKIE
96 Grand Street
New York, NY 10013
(212) 226-4999

ENGLAND

RUPERT GAVENDISH
London, England
01-736-6024

HERMITAGE
London, England
01-730-1973

SPINK AND SON, LTD.
King Street
London, England
SW1Y 6QS

GERMANY

THOMAS POLLER KUNSTHANDEL
Kirchnerstrasse 1-3
D-6000 Frankfurt AM
Main 1
West Germany
069-285269

CONTEMPORARY

BAKER, KNAPP, AND
TUBBS
200 Lexington Avenue
New York, NY 10016
(212) 599-4300

BALLARD DESIGNS
2148-J Hills Avenue
Atlanta, GA
(404) 351-5099

BONAVENTURE FUR-
NITURE INDUSTRIES,
LTD.
894 Bloomfield Avenue
Montreal, Quebec
Canada H2V 3S6
(514) 270-7311

BRUNSCHWIG & FILS
979 Third Avenue
New York, NY 10022
(212) 838-7878

BUCCELLATI INC.
46 East 57th Street
New York, NY 10022
(212) 308-2900

CASA BIQUE, LTD.
P.O. Box 788
500 Carolina Avenue
Thomasville, NC 27360
(919) 472-7700

CASA STRADIVARI
200 Lexington Avenue
New York, NY 10016
(212) 684-5990

CENTURY
160 Fifth Avenue
New York, NY 10010
(212) 989-1180

CLODAGH, ROSS, AND
WILLIAMS
122 St. Marks Place
New York, NY 10003
(212) 505-1774

DONGHIA FURNITURE
979 Third Avenue
New York, NY 10022
(212) 925-2777

GRANGE
Caleche Collection
200 Lexington Avenue
New York, NY 10016
(212) 685-9057

GREENBAUM
COLLECTION
101 Washington Street
Paterson, NJ 07505
(201) 279-3000
(201) 766-5000

P.E. GUERIN
23 Jane Street
New York, NY 10014
(212) 243-5270

HAVILAND & CO., INC.
Bergdorf Goodman
754 Fifth Avenue
New York, NY 10022
(212) 753-7300

HENREDON FURNI-
TURE COMPANY
P.O. Box 70
Morganton, NC 28655
(704) 437-5261

HICKORY FURNITURE
COMPANY
Hickory, NC 28603
(919) 841-8290

JEFFCO
One North Broadway
White Plains, NY 10601
(914) 682-0303

LEE JOFA
979 Third Avenue
New York, NY 10022
(212) 688-0444

KOHLER CO.
Design Center
Kohler, WI 53044
(414) 457-4441

KPS INC.
200 Lexington Avenue
New York, NY 10016
(212) 686-7784

LES PRISMATIQUES
232 East 59th Street
New York, NY 10022
(212) 832-8107

LUTEN CLAREY
STERN, INC.
1059 Third Avenue
Fourth Floor
New York, NY 10021
(212) 838-6420

MARTEX
1221 Sixth Avenue
New York, NY 10020
(212) 382-5185

MASTERWORKS
P.O. Box M
Marietta, Georgia 30061
(404) 423-9000

MILARI
136 East 57th Street
Second Floor
New York, NY 10022
(212) 319-4400

PALAZZETTI
215 Lexington Avenue
New York, NY 10016
(212) 684-1199

SWID POWELL
55 East 57th Street
Fifth Floor
New York, NY 10022
(212) 308-1710

ROSECORE CARPET
CO., INC.
979 Third Avenue
New York, NY 10022
(212) 421-7272

SALADINO FURNI-
TURE INC.
305 East 63rd Street
Fourteenth Floor
New York, NY 10021
(212) 838-0500

SARRIED LTD.
P.O. Box 3548
Wilson, NC 27894
(919) 291-1414

SMITH & WATSON
305 East 63rd Street
New York, NY 10021
(212) 355-5615

WILLIAM ELLIS SMITH
STUDIO
1947 Caherenga Boulevard
Los Angeles, CA 90068
(213) 464-4644

STARK CARPET CO.
979 Third Avenue
New York, NY 10022
(212) 752-9000

STEUBEN GLASS
715 Fifth Avenue (56th
Street)
New York, NY 10022
(212) 752-1441

STROHEIM &
ROMANN, INC.
155 East 56th Street
New York, NY 10022
(212) 691-0700

SUNAR
730 Fifth Avenue
Sixth Floor
New York, NY 10019
(212) 246-5200

TIFFANY & CO.
727 Fifth Avenue
New York, NY 10022
(212) 755-8000

URBAN BOB-KAT
130 Spring Street
New York, NY 10012
(212) 925-7170

URBAN WOODS
37 Main Street
Fulton Landing
Brooklyn, NY 11201
(718) 875-9663

SHERLE WAGNER
60 East 57th Street
New York, NY 10022
(212) 758-3300

JOHN WIDDICOMB
CO.
979 Third Avenue
New York, NY 10022
(212) 421-1200

WORTHINGTON
GROUP LTD.
Merchandise Mart
Twelfth Floor
Atlanta, GA
(404) 872-1608

ARCHITECTS AND
DESIGNERS

JEAN PAUL BEAUJARD
209 East 76th Street
New York, NY 10021
(212) 249-3790

WARD BENNETT
1 West 72nd Street
New York, NY 10023
(212) 580-1358

BILHUBER, INC.
19 East 65th Street
New York, NY 10021
(212) 517-7673

VICTORIA BORUS
DESIGN
111 Wooster Street
New York, NY 10012
(212) 431-4908

SAMUEL BOTERO
150 East 58th Street
New York, NY 10022
(212) 935-5155

RONALD BRICKE
333 East 69th Street
New York, NY 10021
(212) 472-9006

TOM BRITT
15 East 63rd Street
New York, NY 10021
(212) 753-4430

MARIO BUATTA
120 East 80th Street
New York, NY 10021
(212) 988-6811

PETER CARLSON
Carlson Gevis
196 Grand Street
New York, NY 10013
(212) 925-2173

GEORGE CONSTANT
425 East 63rd Street
New York, NY 10021
(212) 751-1907

ROBERT CURRIE
109 West 27th Street,
Room 9E
New York, NY 10001
(212) 206-0505

CHARLES DAMGA
INTERIOR DESIGN
812 Broadway, Second
Floor
New York, NY 10003
(212) 533-8555

ROBERT DENNING
AND VINCENT
FOURCADE INC.
125 East 73rd Street
New York, NY 10021
(212) 759-1969

RUBEN DE SAAVEDRA
225 East 57th Street
New York, NY 10022
(212) 759-2892

MICHAEL DE SANTIS
1110 Second Avenue
New York, NY 10022
(212) 753-8871

DONGHIA ASSOCIATES
315 East 62nd Street
New York, NY 10021
(212) 838-9100

D'URSO DESIGN INC.
80 West 40th Street
New York, NY 10018
(212) 869-9313

MELVIN DWORK INC.
405 East 56th Street, 11N
New York, NY 10022
(212) 759-9330

DAVID EASTON
323 East 58th Street
New York, NY 10022
(212) 486-6701

ANNE EISENHOWER
790 Madison Avenue
New York, NY 10021
(212) 288-3390

FOX AND NAHEM
DESIGN
69 Fifth Avenue
New York, NY 10003
(212) 929-1485

SUZIE FRANKFURT
122 East 73rd Street
New York, NY 10021
(212) 288-9611

STANLEY J. FRIEDMAN
131 Spring Street
New York, NY 10012
(212) 431-3309

RICHARD GILLETTE
144 West 27th Street
New York, NY 10001
(212) 226-3850

MARIETTE HIMES
GOMEZ
241 East 78th Street
New York, NY 10021
(212) 288-6865

MICHAEL GRAVES
341 Nassau Street
Princeton, NJ 08540
(609) 924-6409

CAROLYN GUTTILA
Box 670
Locust Valley, NY 11560
(516) 671-9280

GARY HAGER
Parish-Hadley Associates
305 East 63rd Street
New York, NY 10021
(212) 888-7979

ANTHONY HAIL
1055 California Street
San Francisco, CA 94108
(415) 928-3500

MARK HAMPTON
654 Madison Avenue
New York, NY 10021
(212) 753-4110

ROBERT S. HART
237 East 54th Street
New York, NY 10022
(212) 223-0384

HAWKINSON +
SMITH-MILLER,
ARCHITECTS
305 Canal Street
New York, NY 10013
(212) 966-3875

HOBBS ARCHITEC-
TURE GROUP
110 Union Street, Suite 500
Seattle, WA 98101
(206) 467-8838

HUTCHINGS-LYLE
255 East 72nd Street
New York, NY 10021
(212) 288-2729

IRVINE AND FLEMING
INC.
19 East 57th Street
New York, NY 10022
(212) 888-6000

DAVID L. JAMES
200 Lexington Avenue
New York, NY 10016
(212) 684-3760

NOEL JEFFREY
22 East 65th Street
New York, NY 10021
(212) 535-0300

KISER, GUTLON,
QUINTAL
29 East 10th Street
New York, NY 10003

MICHAEL KRIEGER
45-17 21st Street
Long Island City, NY 11101
(718) 706-0077

MICHAEL LA ROCCA
150 East 58th Street
Suite 3510
New York, NY 10155
(212) 755-5558

JACK LENOR LARSON
232 East 59th Street
New York, NY 10022
(212) 674-3993

DAVID LAURANCE
345 East 57th Street
New York, NY 10022
(212) 752-1152

LEMEAU AND LLANA
325 Bleecker Street
New York, NY 10014
(212) 675-5190

ROBERT K. LEWIS
699 Madison Avenue
New York, NY 10021
(212) 755-1557

MIMI LONDON
8687 Melrose, Suite 151
Los Angeles, CA 90069
(213) 855-2567

STEPHEN MALLORY
170 East 61st Street
New York, NY 10021
(212) 826-6350

KEVIN McNAMARA
541 East 72nd Street
New York, NY 10021
(212) 861-0808

RICHARD MEIER
136 East 57th Street
New York, NY 10022
(212) 967-6060

ROBERT METZGER
210 East 58th Street
New York, NY 10022
(212) 759-0876

JUAN PABLO
MOLYNEUX
29 East 69th Street
New York, NY 10021
(212) 628-0097
or
35 East 67th Street
New York, NY 10021
(212) 737-3933

JUAN MONTOYA
80 Eighth Avenue
New York, NY 10011
(212) 242-3622

JOHN ROBERT
MOORE II
136 East 82nd Street
New York, NY 10028
(212) 249-9370

SANDRA NUNNERLY
400 East 55th Street
New York, NY 10022
(212) 593-1497

PARISH-HADLEY
ASSOCIATES
305 East 63rd Street
New York, NY 10021
(212) 888-7979

PATINO AND WOLF
ASSOCIATES
400 East 52nd Street
New York, NY 10022
(212) 355-6581
(212) 759-7623

ALBERT PENSIS
200 Lexington Avenue
New York, NY 10016
(212) 686-1788

RED ROOF DESIGNS
30 East 20th Street
New York, NY 10003
(212) 598-0360

RICHARD L. RIDGE
903 Park Avenue
New York, NY 10021
(212) 472-0608

TONY RYAN
INTERIORS
160 West 73rd Street
New York, NY 10023
(212) 873-8107

JOHN SALADINO
305 East 63rd Street
New York, NY 10021
(212) 752-2440

RENNY SALTZMAN
815 Fifth Avenue
New York, NY 10021
(212) 753-8861

PAUL SEGAL
730 Fifth Avenue
New York, NY 10019
(212) 247-7440

SHATTUCK BLAIR
ASSOCIATES
315 West 78th Street
New York, NY 10024
(212) 595-0203

SHELTON-MINDEL
ASSOCIATES
216 West 18th Street
New York, NY 10011
(212) 243-3939

MARK SIMON
Centerbrook
P.O. Box 409
Essex, CT 06426
(203) 767-0101

JAY SPECTRE, INC.
964 Third Avenue, Fourth
Floor
New York, NY 10022

ROBERT STERN
200 West 72nd Street
New York, NY 10023
(212) 246-1980

STANLEY TIGERMAN
444 North Wells
Chicago, IL 60610
(312) 644-5880

ROBERT VENTURI
VENTURI, RAUCH,
AND SCOTT-BROWN
4236 Main Street
Philadelphia, PA 19127

LEILA AND MASSIMO
VIGNELLI
410 East 62nd Street
New York, NY 10021
(212) 593-1416

INDEX